Vintage

{ CHRISTMAS CRAFTS }

Vintage
CHRISTMAS CRAFTS

Sara Toliver

Sterling Publishing Co., Inc. New York
A Sterling/Chapelle Book

Chapelle, Ltd.:
 Jo Packham
 Sara Toliver
 Cindy Stoeckl

 Editor: Lecia Monsen
 Art Director: Karla Haberstich
 Copy Editors: Anne Bruns, Marilyn Goff
 Graphic Illustrator: Kim Taylor
 Staff: Kelly Ashkettle, Areta Bingham,
 Donna Chambers, Emily Frandsen, Susan Jorgensen,
 Jennifer Luman, Melissa Maynard, Barbara Milburn,
 Suzy Skadburg, Desirée Wybrow

Library of Congress Cataloging-in-Publication Data

Toliver, Sara.
Vintage Christmas crafts / Sara Toliver.
       p. cm.
"A Sterling/Chapelle Book."
Includes index.
ISBN 1-4027-1604-4
1. Christmas decorations--United States. 2. Interior dec-
oration--United States. I. Title.
TT900.C4T6523 2004
745.594'12--dc22

2004009802

10 9 8 7 6 5 4 3 2 1
Published by Sterling Publishing Co., Inc.
387 Park Avenue South, New York, NY 10016
©2004 by Sara Toliver
Distributed in Canada by Sterling Publishing
c/o Canadian Manda Group, One Atlantic Avenue, Suite 105
Toronto, Ontario, Canada M6K 3E7
Distributed in Great Britain by Chrysalis Books Group PLC,
The Chrysalis Building, Bramley Road, London W10 6SP,
England
Distributed in Australia by Capricorn Link (Australia) Pty. Ltd.
P. O. Box 704, Windsor, NSW 2756, Australia
Printed and Bound in China
All Rights Reserved

Sterling ISBN 1-4027-1604-4

If you have any questions or comments, please contact:
 Chapelle, Ltd., Inc., P.O. Box 9252, Ogden, UT 84409
 (801) 621-2777 • (801) 621-2788 Fax
 e-mail: chapelle@chapelleltd.com
 Web site: www.chapelleltd.com

Space would not permit the inclusion of every decorative item photographed for this book, nor could all of
the designers be identified. Many of these items are
available by contacting:
 Ruby & Begonia, 204 25th Street, Ogden, UT 84401
 (801) 334-7829 • (888) 888-7829 Toll-free
 e-mail: ruby@rubyandbegonia.com
 Web site: www.rubyandbegonia.com

Due to the limited amount of space available, we
must print our patterns at a reduced size in order to
give our patrons the maximum number of patterns
possible in our publications. We believe the quality and
quantity of our patterns will compensate for any incon-
venience this may cause.

This volume is meant to stimulate craft ideas. If read-
ers are unfamiliar or not proficient in a skill necessary
to attempt a project, we urge that they refer to an
instructional book specifically addressing the required
technique.

Lunch

Friture de poisson

Escaloppes de Veau nat...
pommes paysanne

Viande froide assort...

Salade

Fromage – Fruits

WINDSOR.

Her Majesty's Dinner
Monday 17th Decr 1894

Potage
Au Vermicelli à la Windsor
à la Paysanne

Poissons
La Barbue sauce Hollandaise
Les Filets d'Hugrefin frit

Entrées
Les Croquettes de Volaille
La Mousse de Grouse au fumet

Relevé
Roast Beef (Champignons étuvés)

Rôt
Les Canards sauvages sce Bigarade

Entremets
La Chicorée à la Crème
Les Beignets d'Ananas
Le Pain de Pommes ... Chantilly
Cheese Straws

Side Table
Hot & Cold Fowl. Tongue. Cold Beef

Menu

Potage Carmen
Olives – Anchois. Concombres.
Saumon Sauce Hollandaise
...let au Vent à la Financière
Filet de Boeuf Jardinière
Sorbet
Perdreaux Rôtis
Salade
Petits Pois à la Française
Gâteaux   Paquitas
Fruits

MENU

16 Mai 1892

Menu

Contents

Introduction

There is something magical about the Christmas season—the comfort of being at home, of sitting in front of a cozy fireplace drinking hot chocolate and reminiscing about Christmases past. It is a time for family and friends to gather and celebrate together, keeping old traditions and starting new ones.

Decorating with vintage Christmas themes is one way to evoke nostalgia and rekindle the memories that make this time of year so precious. Creating a home filled with interesting details like hand-stitched stockings, lovely painted ornaments, and beautifully wrapped presents can make what is already an extraordinary time into a season that is truly memorable. This book will show you how to find, use, and create antique items in ways you may not have thought of before. It will also show you how new items can be made to look vintage (much of what you'll see in this book is made from new and current craft supplies). You'll find projects ranging from antiquing a Victorian mirror to making holiday Treasure Bags, with step-by-step instructions for making the holiday of your dreams into a fabulous reality.

I am excited to share some of my favorite ideas and designs with you. As you read, pay close attention to the photographs—many of the projects you'll see can be adapted or used differently than what we've shown. The important thing is to design with a personal touch, and to let the spirit of the season inspire you to create truly personal and expressive works of holiday art.

Country
VINTAGE

Decorating with a Country Vintage Style at Christmas means using handmade pieces fashioned after those our grandparents may have used when decorating for the holidays. They are homemade decorations created around the kitchen table, using items that can be found in the kitchen cupboard or an old quilt chest. Each item is simply made and filled with homespun memories.

White Country Christmas

A White Country Christmas conjures up images of snow falling outside by the creek while inside everything is warm and welcoming by the fireplace.

Above: An etched vase adds a frosty note. See pages 74–75 for instructions to make your own etched-glass Christmas decoration.

Above Right: A star made of pearls is another vintage design that adds to a White Christmas theme. See pages 58–59 for instructions.

To create the same White Country Christmas feeling in your home, decorate predominantly in white. To keep everything warm and cozy, use candles, vintage memorabilia and quilts as tablecloths or arranged casually over a chair to be used while singing carols and reading stories. Add flowers and fruit that could have been carefully selected at a country store. Serve simple comfort food that Grandma would have made in her own kitchen.

Angel Party

Decorate the entire house with handmade white snow angels. Purchase these at country fairs and farmer's markets or have an angel party a few weeks before the holidays begin. Invite all of your friends and ask them to bring a handwritten copy of their favorite angel story. When they arrive, have two tables set for guests. Fill one with an abundance of food and drink. Supply the other with all of the items that may be needed for everyone to make their own angel. For inspiration and help, have angel pictures torn from magazines, vintage postcards with angels, or favorite children's books with heavenly angels. Use pieces of cotton, yards of lace, wooden heads, architectural elements, and wings cut from pieces of rusted tin to complete the angels. At the end of the day, each guest can display their angel and read their story.

Candle Vase

Cast a warm, intimate glow over the holidays with a Candle Vase. As a gift, these can be personalized for each recipient simply by choosing different wallpaper.

- Acrylic decorating paste, 4 oz.
- Acrylic paint, coordinating color
- Craft scissors
- Cake decorating disposable bag, with coupler
- Cake decorating tip #13
- Dish soap
- Glass cylinder vase
- Glitter
- Paintbrush
- Pillar candle
- Reverse decoupage glue
- Wallpaper scrap

1. Using dish soap and water, clean vase and allow to dry.

2. Trim wallpaper to fit the inside of vase. Brush a thin layer of reverse decoupage glue onto the front of wallpaper. Adhere to inside of the vase.

3. Add enough acrylic paint to half a jar of decorating paste for a coordinating tint.

4. Fill decorating bag one-third full with tinted decorating paste. Using the photograph above as a guide, write name or phrase and draw a border onto vase.

5. Immediately sprinkle glitter over decorating paste and allow to dry thoroughly overnight.

6. Place pillar candle in vase.

Holiday Houses

The little houses shown in the photograph on pages 16–17 have been popular, in one form or another, for over a hundred years. Using the photographs as a guide and the instructions on pages 18–21, they are easy to make and can be used in a scene on the mantel, under the tree, or as decorations on a wreath. With your children, make one or more houses to add to your collection each year. Use the date as the address above the door and build your village. When they leave home, they can take the houses they built as the beginning of a village and tradition of their own.

Materials are for one house.

- Acrylic paints, assorted colors
- Batting
- Chipboard
- Cellophane tape
- Clear acetate sheeting
- Craft knife
- Craft scissors
- Ivory pipe cleaner (2)
- Paintbrushes
- Paper cup
- Pencil
- Pine garland, mini strand
- Ruler
- Sand, assorted colors (small packages)
- Scrap paper
- Transfer paper
- White bottle-brush trees, small (3)
- White craft glue
- White crystal glitter
- Vintage mica snow
- White permanent marker

House Colors and Textures

Red House Paint Colors:

- Base: white
- House: brick red
- Roof: gray
- Shutters and balcony: black

Red House Textures:

- Base: white crystal glitter
- House, excluding balcony and shutters: sand mixture of black, red, tan
- Roof: vintage mica snow
- Tree: white acrylic paint

Blue House Paint Colors:

- Base, fences, and shutters: white
- House: blue
- Roofs: navy blue

Blue House Textures:

- Base: white crystal glitter
- House, excluding balcony and shutters: sand mixture of black, dark blue, light blue, crystal glitter
- Roof: vintage mica snow
- Tree: white acrylic paint

Green House Paint Colors:

- Base and fences: white
- House: green
- Roof: forest green
- Shutters and balcony: brick red

Green House Textures:

- Base: white crystal glitter
- House, excluding balcony and shutters: sand mixture of crystal glitter, dark green, light green
- Roof: vintage mica snow
- Tree: white acrylic paint

General House Assembly

1. Enlarge and photocopy *House Patterns* on pages 19–21. Transfer onto chipboard and cut out sections with a craft knife.

2. For windows, cut along the top, bottom, and through the center. Mark score lines on wrong side of chipboard, score along dotted lines to fold back the shutters.

3. Trace outline of each window onto acetate sheeting. Draw panes inside the outline of windows with a white permanent marker.

4. Trim acetate windows with scissors, leaving approximately ¼" allowance on all sides. Adhere acetate windows to inside openings of house with craft glue.

5. Paint all house pieces and allow to dry.

6. Apply craft glue to one portion of house at a time. Using a paper cup, mix sand and pour over glued portion. Let sit for one minute. Tap extra sand onto scrap paper, roll and pour sand back into cup. Repeat for all sides.

7. Construct house, using craft glue and a paintbrush, following assembly instructions for individual house. Reinforce pieces on wrong sides with cellophane tape as needed during construction.

Red House

1. Place *Base (A)* on a flat surface. Centering on rear and ½" in from edge, glue *Back (B)* to *Base (A)*.

2. Glue one *Side (C)* to both *Base (A)* and each side to *Back (B)*.

3. Fold around and glue *Balcony (1)* to *Balcony (2)*.

4. Glue completed balcony under top-left window on *Front (D)*.

5. Glue *Front (D)* to both *Base (A)* and *Sides (C)*.

6. Glue *Roof (E)* onto house with notched edges interlocking with base of peaks.

7. Glue *Roof (F)* to *Roof (E)* creating gables of top windows of *Front (D)*.

8. With craft glue, adhere batting to house front to make a snow drift, referring to photograph on pages 16–17 for placement. Paint white and add crystal glitter.

9. Using craft glue, adhere bottle-brush tree to *Base (A)* and ivory pipe cleaner as a garland to *Front (D)*.

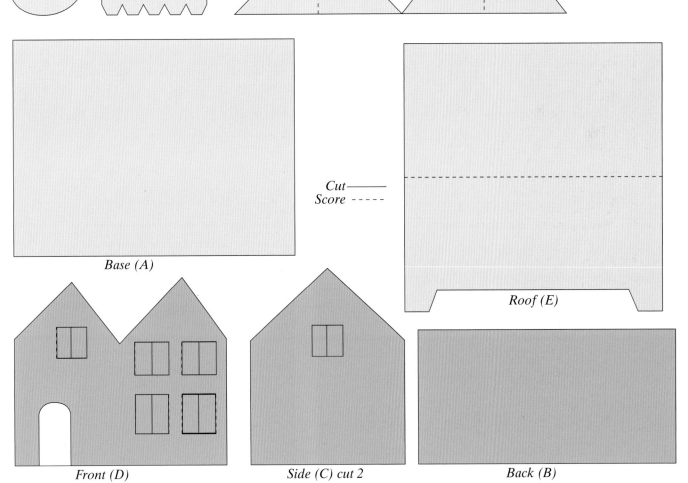

Balcony (2)

Balcony (1)

Roof (F)

Red House Pattern
Enlarge 220%

Base (A)

Cut ———
Score - - - - -

Roof (E)

Front (D)

Side (C) cut 2

Back (B)

19

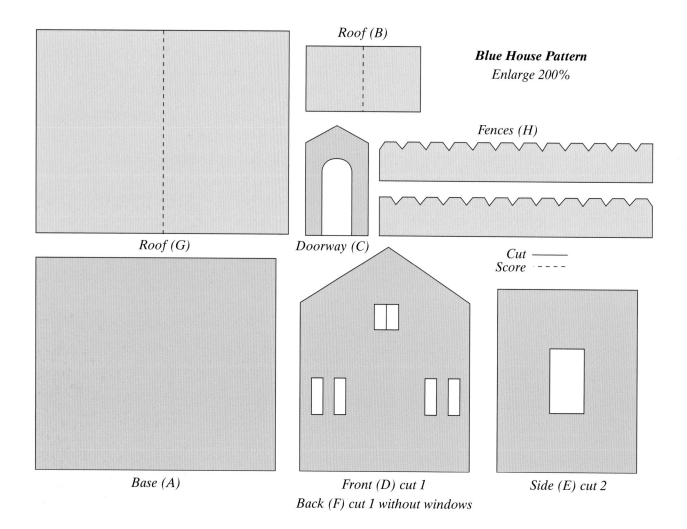

Roof (B)

Blue House Pattern
Enlarge 200%

Fences (H)

Roof (G)

Doorway (C)

Cut ——————
Score - - - - -

Base (A)

Front (D) cut 1
Back (F) cut 1 without windows

Side (E) cut 2

Blue House

1. Place *Base (A)* on a flat surface.

2. Glue *Roof (B)* to top of *Doorway (C)*.

3. Glue completed *Doorway (C)* to *Front (D)*.

4. Center and glue *Front (D)* on *Base (A)* with doorway against edge of *Base (A)*.

5. Glue *Side (E)* to *Base (A)* and *Front (D)*.

6. Glue *Back (F)* to *Base (A)* and *Sides (E)*.

7. Place and glue *Roof (G)* to house.

8. Glue *Fences (H)* to *Base (A)* on corners, placing smaller ends in front of house.

9. With craft glue, adhere batting to house to make a snow drift, referring to photograph on page 18 for placement. Paint white and add crystal glitter.

10. Using craft glue, adhere bottle-brush tree to *Base (A)* and mini pine garland to *Front (D)*.

Green House

1. Place *Base (A)* on a flat surface.

2. Center and glue *Back (B)* on rear edge of *Base (A)*.

3. Place and glue *Sides (C)* to *Back (B)* and to *Base (A)*.

4. Score along dotted lines and fold *Doorway (E)*.

5. Position *Balcony Floor (D)* inside *Doorway (E)*, 1" from top and glue.

6. Glue completed *Doorway (E)* on *Front (F)*.

7. Glue *Front (F)* to *Sides (C)* and *Base (A)*.

8. Glue *Roof (G)* on top of house with notched edges interlocking at base of peak.

9. Glue *Roof (B)* to *Roof (G)*, creating a gable over center window of *Front (F)*.

10. Glue *Fences (H)* to *Base (A)* on corners, placing shorter ends in front of the house.

11. Using craft glue, adhere bottle-brush tree to *Base (A)*, mini pine garland, and ivory pipe cleaner wreath to *Front (F)*, referring to photograph on page 18 for placement.

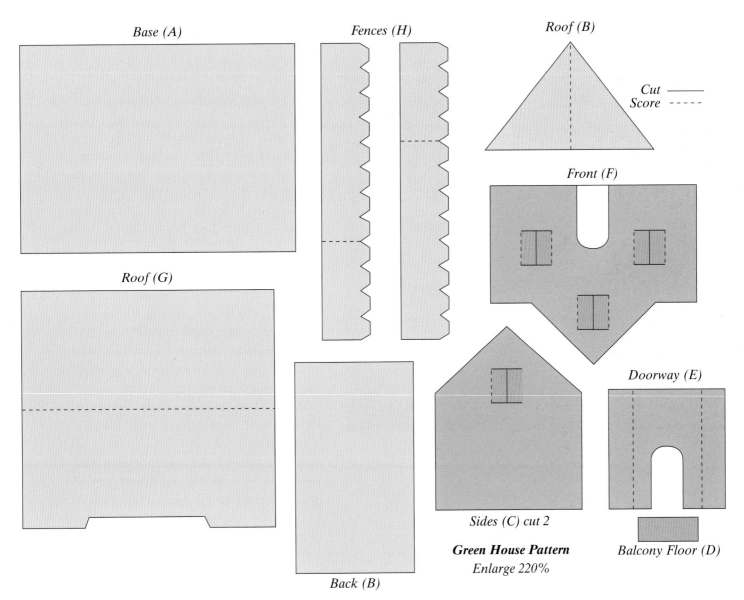

Base (A)

Fences (H)

Roof (B)

Cut ———
Score - - - - -

Front (F)

Roof (G)

Doorway (E)

Sides (C) cut 2

Back (B)

Balcony Floor (D)

Green House Pattern
Enlarge 220%

Collections

Country Vintage Style means decorating with collections. These collections are often handmade decorations that are given to or received from family and friends as gifts.

Above: Collections are often used to decorate the home, sometimes where decorations are not normally found. Guests may have to be careful when sitting to put on winter boots and coats.

Above Right: Simple star shapes, cut from manila file folders, are embellished with paper elements and charms. Each year, new ornaments are made to commemorate special happenings during the year and added to the previous year's collection.

Painted Gourd Party

Christmas is all about celebrating, memories, and collecting, so create a special memory and a new collection by starting before Thanksgiving. Visit a farmer's market and choose two gourds for each guest. At home, wash the gourds thoroughly with hot water, mild dish soap and a few drops of bleach. Do not be afraid to scrub to remove the dirt. Allow gourds to "cure" or dry for several weeks. To shorten this time, purchase precured gourds from a craft store.

Send invitations to family and friends for a gourd-decorating party early in the holiday season. The invitation could contain ideas for decorating the gourds. Each person could paint a gourd to resemble themselves, thus creating an entire family for the mantel. Everyone could choose a favorite holiday character as inspiration for their gourd or simply paint the gourds with designs such as stars, snowflakes, holly, or other holiday images. Provide tables covered with newspaper and supplies to decorate the dry gourds. Include stencils, border stickers, buttons, and pictures of painted gourds from magazines. These can help individuals that may be a bit insecure about their design abilities. Once the gourd is painted and dry, preserve it, using an acrylic sealer, floor wax, or water-based varnish.

Decorating with Collections

To design a Vintage Country Christmas, decorations are created from household items and children's toys. A rocking horse can be set next to the tree with a small holly wreath hanging from the neck. A child's smaller dolls can decorate the branches of the tree and larger baby dolls can be dressed in holiday finery and put among the packages underneath. The beautiful, delicate dolls can be dressed in white, with small wings made from feathers stitched to the back of the dress, and used as angels. A toy barn and farm animals can be used to build a manger for the wise men. When there are children or grandchildren in the house, there is really no need to buy decorations for the holidays. They love to have their favorites all dressed up and put where everyone can see them.

For decoration or gift giving, vintage-style hatboxes can be made, filled with gifts, and stacked in the corner of the room to wait for Christmas morning. It is a wonderful surprise when the package itself becomes part of the gift because these special wrappings can be taken home and used again.

Decorative Boxes

Beautiful packages can be made by covering papier-mâché boxes with old wallpaper, wrapping paper, or a collage of Christmas cards and other holiday memorabilia.

Hatboxes or bandboxes, such as those shown in the large photograph on pages 24–25 are very collectible. Good substitutes are available at most crafts stores and are easily embellished with a variety of techniques, including those that follow.

Papier-mâché boxes can be given a vintage flair like the purchased heart-shaped papier-mâché box shown in the small photograph on page 25. To make this gift box, lightly wash wrapping paper, enough to cover the box, with watered-down brown acrylic paint and let dry. If wrinkled, press with an iron. Trace outlines of the box top, bottom, and sides by placing it on the wrong side of the washed wrapping paper and drawing around it. Cut out pieces, allowing an overlap for good coverage. Adhere paper to box, using decoupage glue painted on the outside of the box. Gently smooth out any wrinkles, being careful not to get glue on the right side of the paper. Allow to dry.

Make a folded gift box like the one on the opposite page, top right, using the **Box Pattern**, below, by enlarging and copying the pattern onto cardstock. Cover the outside of the box, using iron-on webbing to adhere paper of choice to cardstock. Then simply fold and glue in place, using a glue stick. Another option is to use a box you like the shape of as a pattern. Unfold the box and trace the outline onto a manila file folder. Be certain to mark the folds on the new box form. For a larger box, use a piece of posterboard.

For a more unusual gift box, paint a purchased papier-mâché boot like the one on the bottom left of the opposite page, with acrylic paints. Paint the boot red and the cuff white. Dry-brush a small amount of white on the red part of the boot for snow. Wash the boot with a watered-down brown acrylic to add a sense of age. Allow to dry. Brush clear-drying glue on large patches of the boot including the white parts. Sprinkle glitter over glue and let dry.

Embellish a small jewelry gift box as shown on the opposite page, top left. Cut a scene from a vintage Christmas card to match the top of the box. Adhere with glue and allow to dry. Tie a bow around the box with coordinating ribbon.

Use old storage boxes as another type of gift box. The packaging boxes that vintage toys or Christmas decorations used to come in like the one, opposite page bottom right, make wonderful gift boxes for friends who love anything vintage.

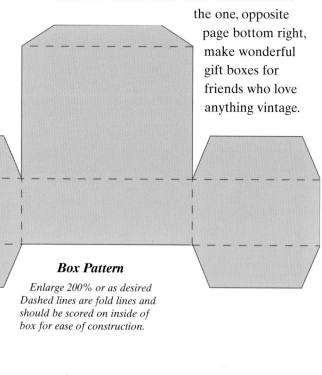

Box Pattern

*Enlarge 200% or as desired
Dashed lines are fold lines and
should be scored on inside of
box for ease of construction.*

Cut ——————
Score - - - - -

26

Yuletide Cottages

These little cottages, very popular in the '50s, were copied from original Victorian ornaments and then mass-produced and imported from the Orient. They are still plentiful in antique stores, but if the colors are wrong or you cannot find any in useable condition, you can make your own.

- Acrylic paints: light blue, green, pink, white
- Cardboard
- Chipboard
- Craft glue
- Craft knife
- Foam brushes (3)
- Glitter: gold, white
- Green bottle-brush trees, small (2)
- Pencil
- Red acetate sheeting
- Ruler
- Scissors
- Transfer paper
- Vintage mica snow

General Cottage Assembly

1. Photocopy *House Patterns* on pages 29–31. Transfer cottage pieces onto chipboard and cut out sections with a craft knife. Cut base from cardboard using craft knife.

2. Mark score lines on wrong side of chipboard. Score along dotted lines.

3. Paint all pieces, referring to photograph above as a guide. While still wet, sprinkle with a small amount of white glitter and allow to dry thoroughly.

4. Cut acetate with scissors to fit doorways and windows. Adhere onto inside of cottage with craft glue.

5. Adhere gold glitter and vintage mica snow to roof and base with craft glue.

6. Brush white acrylic paint onto trees for a fresh snow appearance.

7. Construct cottage, using craft glue and a paintbrush, following assembly instructions for individual cottage. Reinforce pieces on wrong sides with cellophane tape as needed during construction.

Blue House

1. Fold *House (A)* along scored lines, gluing where right side overlaps onto the back.

2. Fold *Roof over door (B)* along scored line and glue onto *House (A)*, placing over door.

3. Fold *Roof (C)* along scored lines, centering and gluing over house.

4. Place *Platform (D)* onto a flat surface.

5. Center and glue house on rear edge of *Platform (D)*.

Blue House Pattern
Pattern is actual size

Platform (D)

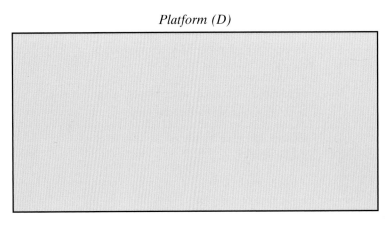

Roof (C)

Cut ———
Score ‐ ‐ ‐ ‐

Roof over door (B)

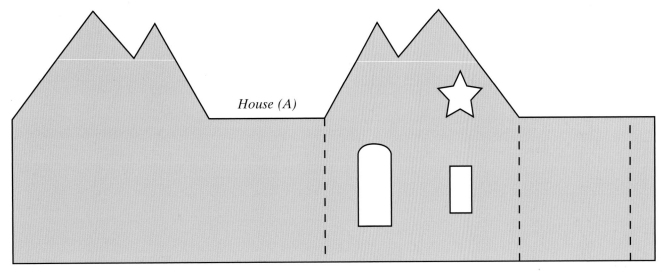

House (A)

Green House

1. Fold *House (A)* along scored lines, gluing where right side overlaps onto back.

2. Fold *Chimney (B)* along scored lines, gluing where right side overlaps onto back.

3. Glue *Chimney (B)* on rear-right side of *House (A)*, aligning edge of chimney to house.

4. Fold *Roof (C)* along scored lines. Align with rear edge of house and glue.

5. Center and glue house on the rear edge of *Platform (D)*.

6. Attach one tree to right-front corner of *Platform (D)* by twisting bottom into cardboard.

Pattern is actual size

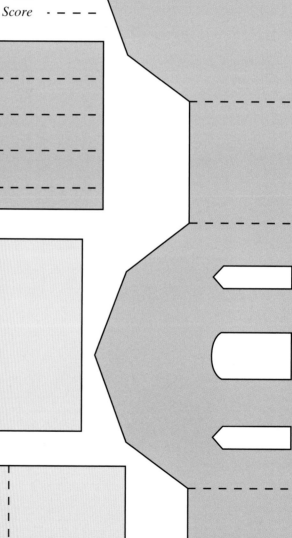

House (A)

Cut ——————
Score - - - -

Chimney (B)

Platform (D)

Roof (C)

30

Pink House

1. Fold *House (A)* along scored lines, gluing where right side overlaps onto back.

2. Fold *Roof Left (B)* along scored lines and glue to left side of house, aligning and centering crease with house peak.

3. Fold *Roof Right (C)* along scored lines and glue to right side of house, centering crease point to middle of *Roof Left (B)*.

4. Place *Platform (D)* on a flat surface.

5. Center and glue house on rear edge of *Platform (D)*.

6. Attach one Christmas tree to left-front corner of *Platform (D)* by twisting bottom into cardboard.

Pink House Pattern
Pattern is actual size

Platform (D)

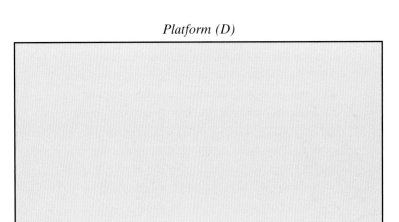

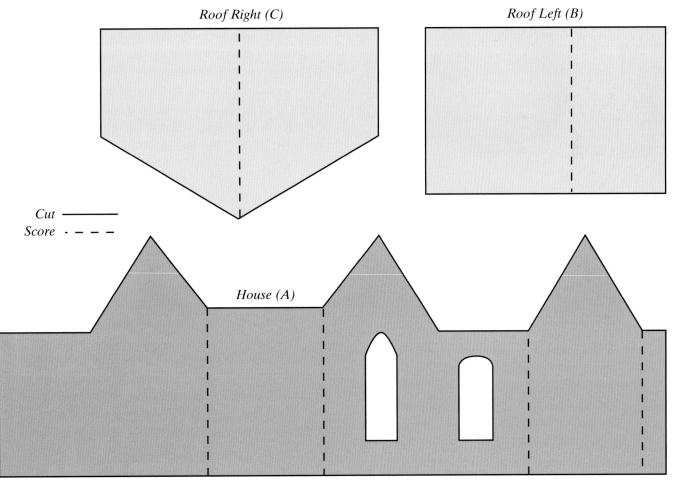

Roof Right (C)

Roof Left (B)

Cut ———

Score · — — —

House (A)

Repurposing Ornaments

Creating small Christmas ornaments can be a snowy-afternoon project for the entire family and create perfect additions to your Christmas collections. Some old ornaments are too worn to hang on the tree by themselves, but can be used to create new ornaments, so they not only become this year's treasures but next year's Christmas tradition. The wreath below was made by simply gluing miniature vintage ornaments together into a circle. Such tiny ornaments can be glued into a number of shapes including a tree, star, or heart. If small children need a pattern, draw one, using a cookie cutter, onto a piece of white butcher paper. Have them glue the ornaments together with a low-temp glue gun, using the drawing as a guide.

The small boot, shown above right, is a '50s ceramic boot painted red, highlighted with gold paint, with a small amount of tea-stained batting glued to the cuff. A small horse and a tiny pine tree were put inside the boot with a red glitter star. Tinsel garland was threaded through a small ornament and hung around the boot top.

Holiday Barnyard

Create a small holiday barnyard by building a fence from small wired garland purchased from a craft store. Use your imagination to create trellises, arches, hidden pathways, and secret gardens. Place small farm animals inside the fence around the base of a Christmas tree or a wooden barn such as a birdhouse brought inside for the winter. Hang miniature wreaths on the door, attach miniature lights (available at craft stores) around the eaves of the roof, set an angel weather vane on the barn cupola, and place small decorated Christmas trees and a collection of country-style Santas among the animals.

When creating this holiday barnyard, shown on opposite page, do not confine yourself to keeping all of the pieces in the same scale. It is much more of a designer statement if a few of the items are larger than the other pieces. The larger items will be the focal point of the vignette so make certain they are pieces that you want attention drawn to. Because this particular barnyard scene is a holiday one, the Christmas tree is much larger than the accent pieces and decorated with nontraditional ornaments such as miniature farm animals and tiny bales of hay. The heart on the top of the tree was made by simply cutting a Christmas card into a heart shape and gluing miniature vintage tinsel around the outside. Use silver braid or antique ribbon in place of the tinsel.

Using Everyday Collections

If you truly enjoy decorating for the holidays but find yourself short of money to buy all of the decorations that you need, consider this solution. Decorate with your favorite everyday collections, such as a Noah's Ark collection, an array of birdhouses, or summer garden statuary.

Leave the existing collections where they are, and simply add something that has a holiday feel. Place a tiny series of decorated trees on the ark, hang wreaths and miniature lights on the birdhouses, or adorn the garden statuary with holly, pinecones, and cranberries.

Use your collections to display gifts that are given to holiday guests. Attach a tag to tiny spruce or pine trees potted in hand-painted Christmas clay pots. Place the trees among one of the vignettes. When family and friends visit, let them select a tree to take home and plant after the snow has melted. This way, your guests will be reminded of a special Christmas memory every month of the year.

Another idea for incorporating everyday collections into the seasonal decor is to make small tags or cards with a Christmas wish or poem written on the back. Tie the tags to small boxes wrapped in brown kraft paper or cup-sized burlap bags filled with things that echo your collections. Use animal crackers if the featured collection is Noah's Ark, or birdseed for birdhouses. A designer secret for making decorations seem extraordinary is to tie the gift-giving into the theme of the home's decor. It wouldn't make sense or be nearly as memorable to give boxes of chocolates wrapped in red paper and gold bows if the home is decorated with vintage Noah's Ark pieces.

An added benefit of decorating with everyday collections is that friends and family may give you a piece to add to your collection each year. It helps them to know that what they buy for you will be truly enjoyed. It adds to memories of the holidays and will be treasured for the entire year.

Dining with Collections

Use collections as part of table decorations during holiday parties. Mimic beautiful hotel buffets by having one table for drinks, silverware, and dishes; one table for salads; one table for main dishes; and one table for desserts. By using separate tables for each course, your home appears to have more decorations than if everything were clustered together around the tree. It is also an opportunity to use special decorations where everyone will notice them. Just make certain that the food is easily reached without disturbing any of the decorative items. It will make your guests uncomfortable and less likely to enjoy the buffet if they are worried about knocking over a fragile decoration.

You can still use collections as decorations at a sit-down dinner. Just be careful not to over-decorate. The centerpieces should be low so guests can talk over them and be evenly spaced down the center of the table so that there is room to place filled serving dishes. If candles are included, make certain that they are dripless and secure in the candleholders so that they do not get knocked over and wax isn't dripped on your treasured pieces.

Natural Christmas

Country decorating is often simple and almost always natural. It is filled with simple garlands made from fragrant pine boughs, centerpieces of fruits and greenery, holly and ivy, freshly baked gingerbread men, and popcorn and berries.

Above: A grouping of primitive Santas are displayed in a window and completed with a garland of pepper berry sprays and pine boughs.

Above Right: A natural swag, embellished with apples and a fresh pineapple, crowns a portrait.

Greenery Garlands

To festoon a banister with natural garland as shown on the opposite page, first measure the length of the banister to determine how long to make the garland. Multiply length by two for average swags. Add or subtract length as desired to adjust swag size. The following procedure can be adapted to create single swags to adorn collections or pictures.

Cut a piece of ½" rope to the desired length adding a 12" length at each end. Wrap one end with 21-gauge florist wire for a space of 3". Strip foliage from the bottom third of the stems of chosen greenery. Starting at the unwrapped end of the rope, hold stems against rope base, tips pointing upward, and wrap wire tightly around rope and stems four to five times. Continue adding greenery, overlapping each addition to hide the wire underneath. Berry or fruit sprays can be added at intervals to embellish garland as desired. Turn garland often to maintain fullness.

Tie rope ends to the newel posts and use floral wire to secure garland to banister at intervals. The heavier the garland, the heavier the wire that will be needed to hold the garland in place. A general rule of thumb is 26-gauge for lighter projects, 21-gauge for middle weight, and 18-gauge for heavy projects. Hide wires that are wrapped around the banister and tied to the newel posts beneath ribbon bows. To maintain a fresh garland, wrap the banister in plastic wrap before hanging the garland and mist it with water daily.

Cranberry Garlands

Cut a piece of fishing line the desired length and tie a button or metal washer to the end to make a stop. Thread a large-eyed needle with the other end of the length of fishing line and pierce frozen cranberries, stringing them onto the line one at a time. Frozen berries are neater and easier to work with. Finish the garland by tying another button or metal washer at the end. Once the holidays are done, simply hang the garland outside for the birds to enjoy. Vary by using dried apple slices and popcorn as separators. Stale popcorn, unsalted and unbuttered, is easier to work with because the kernels do not fall apart as easily. Thread the different elements in a pleasing manner and knot the end of the line to finish.

Fruit Garlands

Embellish simple garlands by adding fruits, vegetables, pinecones, cinnamon sticks, and other natural objects. To make a more elaborate style of garland, follow the directions on page 40, making certain that the rope used for the base is heavier than that used for a simple garland. Increase the amount of greenery to achieve the fullness necessary to support the additional decorative objects.

When you have completed wiring the boughs to the rope, place the finished garland on a long table, counter, or floor and begin to attach the fruit. Insert a floral pick into each piece of fruit or vegetable. Tie the wire end of the pick to the rope base of the garland. If items such as pinecones or cinnamon sticks are included, simply wrap and twist pieces of medium-gauge florist wire around each object and wire to the pine bough base.

These garlands are often very heavy so you may need help when attaching it to the banister. When fresh fruits or vegetables are used, choose items that are underripe. Be certain that the garland is not placed in direct sun, otherwise you will have to replace the fresh items frequently.

When adding bows to the garlands, choose natural-looking bows made from strips of torn cotton, burlap ribbon, or hand-dyed yarns.

43

Garland Parties

Garlands can be made from a number of natural or homemade objects but one of the most enjoyable is gingerbread men. It can be a considerable amount of work to make enough cookies to duplicate the garland pictured at left, or it can be the reason for a holiday party.

Throw a party for your children or grandchildren and invite all of their friends. Supply bowls of cranberries and popcorn for stringing, and everyone can make their own Gingerbread Men from the recipe on page 46. Let each child decorate two or more cookies. Supply a variety of cookie cutters and several small bowls of raisins, beads, buttons, and torn strips of cotton fabric. If they choose to use beads or buttons, make an impression in the dough with the object where it will be glued after baking. Punch a hole in the top of the cookie so that they are easy to attach to the garland. After the cookies are baked and cooled, have the children sign their name and the year on the back of their cookies. Coat the cookies with decoupage medium to preserve them. Save one cookie from each child for your garland and let them take the others home that they decorated.

Another option is to have a cookie party with your own friends. Send out brown paper invitations in the shape of gingerbread men. Ask each guest to make and decorate as many cookies as there will be guests. Include the recipe with the invitation and remind everyone to sign and date the back of their cookies. Set up a large table with empty platters so each guest can arrange and display the cookies that they brought. One of each of the guests' cookies is for the hostess to add to her garland and the other guests are invited to take one of each of the remaining styles home with them for their own garland or tree. As a gift to your guests, decorate flat boxes lined with waxed paper to transport the cookies. Write a message to each guest right on the lid of the box, or draw a gingerbread man and adorn him with buttons and beads and write the guest's name on his tummy.

Gingerbread Men

Note: These ornaments are for decorative purposes only.

- 3 tablespoons shortening
- ½ cup sugar
- ½ cup molasses
- 1 teaspoon baking soda
- 3½ cups flour
- 1 teaspoon cinnamon
- 1 teaspoon cloves
- 1 teaspoon ginger
- ¾ cup water
- Cookie cutter(s) of choice
- Drinking straw
- Clear acrylic varnish

1. Preheat oven to 350°F. Beat shortening and sugar together until light and fluffy; stir in molasses. Sift dry ingredients together and add to shortening mixture with water. Dough will be stiff. Refrigerate overnight.

2. Cut dough into three pieces. Knead dough to warm slightly. Roll out a piece to ¼" thick. Cut out ornaments, using cookie cutter(s).

3. With a drinking straw, punch hole in ornament for hanging. Place on greased cookie sheet and bake 20 minutes. Turn oven off and let cool in oven.

4. Remove ornaments from sheet and place on rack to harden for three days. Preserve with three coats of clear acrylic varnish and allow to dry. Decorate as desired.

Star Cookie Tree

Cookies are a great decorative item. They can be used in many ways, like this sweet tree shown below, "dusted" with snow.

Note: These ornaments are for decorative purposes only.

- ½ cup margarine softened
- ½ cup sugar
- 2–3 teaspoons eggnog extract
- 4 cups all-purpose flour
- Star cookie cutters, 3 sizes
- Purchased frosting
- Clear acrylic varnish

1. Preheat oven to 350°F. In large bowl, mix margarine, sugar, and extract together. Work flour in with hands. If dough is crumbly, add 1–2 tablespoons softened margarine.

2. On a lightly floured surface, roll dough to ½" thickness. Cut shapes from dough, using cookie cutters.

3. Bake on ungreased cookie sheet 15–20 minutes; avoid overbaking smaller cookies. Immediately remove from cookie sheet and cool on wire rack. Preserve cookies with three coats of clear acrylic varnish and allow to dry.

4. Make tree by stacking cookies. Use frosting as glue between each cookie and dollops of frosting on star tips for snow.

Garland Pointers

Garlands can be made small enough to cover just a corner of a picture frame or large enough to encase an entire door frame. When attaching garlands to a wall, use nails large enough to hold the weight of the garland at regular intervals. Avoid choosing nails that are too small or the garland will pull out of the wall. Drive nails into the woodwork in places where the holes will not be seen during the rest of the year. If the garland is hung from molding, put the nail where the molding meets the wall. Tie the garland to the nails with heavy-duty fishing line or medium-gauge wire. If there are strings of lights on the garland, they should be added before attaching it to the wall. Match the garland lights to the decorations in the room. Here the lights are blue to coordinate with the spatterware.

Natural Gifts

Small potted trees or herbs that have been pruned to look like trees, can be used as holiday decorations as well as gifts for family and friends.

Place the plant in a pot and fill to about 2" below the rim of the pot with dirt. Cover the dirt with mood moss and sprinkle tiny pinecones and acorns around the base, or place a series of small rocks that have Christmas words painted on each one on the moss. Use black rub-on letters or metallic paint pens and write one word on each rock. Use words such as Noel, Peace, Hope, Joy, Love, or any others that sound like Christmas.

The best plants to grow for this project are rosemary, thyme, myrtle, angel vine, boxwood, or golden cyprus. These are all easily trimmed to topiary shapes or left as they are to grow and resemble miniature trees.

Natural Decorating Tips

Natural objects can be placed almost any-where in the home on any surface. If they are placed in front of a window or heat source, they may dry out quickly. Ask your florist or gardener if the wreath, garland, or tree you are purchasing will dry well naturally; if it doesn't, make certain that it is watered or misted every day.

Other ideas for backdrops are homemade quilts, bulletin boards, or architectural elements like the shutters on the opposite page.

Treasure Bags

Create lovely packages for Christmas gifts and give two gifts in one. Your gift will be doubly appreciated when it is presented in a lovely bag such as this that can be used after the holiday season.

- Antique lace or doily, 5½" square
- Awl
- Brown/gold ribbon, ⅜" wide (1½ yards)
- Brown woven fabric, 8" square
- Burlap drawstring bag, 9" x 10"
- Disappearing-ink fabric marker
- Embroidery hoop, 6"
- Embroidery needle, large-eyed
- Gold ribbon, ⅛" wide (¾ yard)
- Green/brown rayon ribbon, 1.5mm
- Green rayon cord, thin
- Scissors
- Sewing needle and thread
- Transfer paper

1. Place brown woven fabric in embroidery hoop, transfer *Embroidery Pattern,* opposite page, onto the fabric with fabric marker. Before making each stitch, use an awl to pierce the fabric to create an opening large enough for the ribbon to pass easily through.

2. Embroider the pinecone with brown/gold ribbon and large-eyed embroidery needle, following the instructions for the *Cretan Stitch,* opposite page.

3. Form branch with green/brown ribbon following *Straight Stitch* instructions on opposite page. Add pine needles, using *Straight Stitch* with green cord.

4. Tie a 2½" bow with the gold ribbon and hand-stitch in place at top of branch. One at a time, thread needle with bow ends and *Cascade* ends following the instructions on opposite page.

5. Create a frayed effect by cutting woven material ½" around design edge and pulling loose threads.

6. Center and hand-stitch lace doily to bag front with sewing needle and thread.

7. Center and hand-stitch embroidered fabric to bag front, stitching around design to secure.

Stitch Guide

■ *Cretan Stitch*

Bring needle up at *A* at top of inner stitching line, then down at *B*. Bring needle up at *C*, just right of *D*. Pull stitches loosely into place. *See (1)*. Bring needle up at *E*, on inner stitching line, keeping needle under previous stitch. Go down at *F*, then up at *G*. *See (2)*. Continue stitching in this manner to bottom of pinecone.

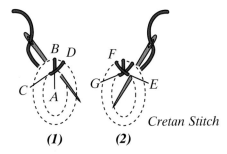

Cretan Stitch

(1)   **(2)**

■ *Straight Stitch*

Bring needle up at *A*. Carry ribbon to desired length of stitch; then go down at *B*.

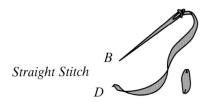

Straight Stitch

■ *Cascade Stitch*

Go down at *A*. *See (1)*. Come up at *B* and go down at *C*, making a small backstitch to hold cascade in place. Come up at *D* underneath the backstitch. *See (2)*. Repeat for remaining stitches in *Embroidery Pattern*.

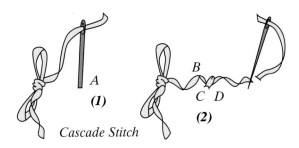

(1)

(2)

Cascade Stitch

■ *Ribbon Stitch*

Bring needle at *A*. Lay the ribbon flat against fabric. Pierce center of ribbon on the way back through fabric at *B* to create a soft curl at end of stitch. Pull ribbon through gently so as not to lose the soft curl.

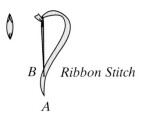

Ribbon Stitch

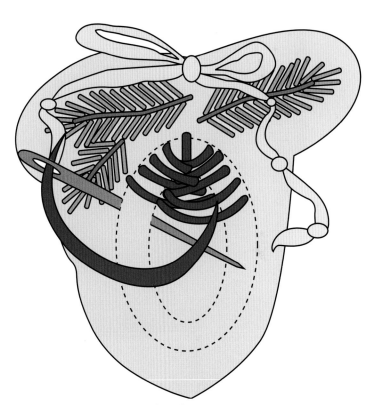

Embroidery Pattern

Shown Actual Size

Chic VINTAGE

A fashionably Chic Vintage Christmas is my mother's favorite style to decorate with for the holidays. She loves everything that looks old but it doesn't necessarily have to be old for her to enjoy it. Sometimes the new ornaments that are fashioned after the old ones are much less expensive and easier to find. She likes to add crystals and layers of tinsel for a touch of elegance to distressed vintage ornaments that are often so simple.

Sparkle and Shimmer

A Chic Vintage Christmas reminds me of department store windows, dressed for the holidays, stopping passersby as they gaze at the wonders inside. The sparkle and shimmer of the trees always seem to catch my eye.

Unique Tannenbaums

A Chic Vintage Christmas is about the glamour and embellishments from days gone by. Garlands of shimmering beads strung on trees and wrapped around banisters give your home a sense of classic finery.

Be creative and try something new this year. Instead of one Christmas tree, have three smaller ones. A grouping of tabletop trees is a unique way to showcase smaller or more fragile ornaments. Place small metallic trees in urns and statuary brought in from the garden. Cover the potted tree base with mica snow or soft angel hair and you are ready to decorate.

Drape beaded garland and tinsel on trees in colors of antique silver, gold, and white. Hang favorite chic ornaments, both old and new. Snow covered stars, glittering snowflakes, and various etched-glass shapes are just a few ideas. These can be purchased or easily handmade. Spend an evening by the fireplace decorating ornaments with sequins, glitter, and other new finds. Brush ornaments with clear-drying craft glue, sprinkle with glitter, mica snow, or other embellishments, and let dry. Create a new hanger by hot-gluing ribbon at the top of the ornament and tie a bow. The sparkle of your decorations will echo the shimmer of the falling snow outside, perfect for this magical time of year.

Tinsel Star

The ornaments on these two pages are all glamourous vintage touches for tree or package decorations.

- Hot-glue gun and glue sticks
- Ornament hanger
- Silver metallic beads (4)
- Silver metallic pipe cleaners (16)
- Wire, 26-gauge (18")
- Wire cutters

1. Cut a pipe cleaner into thirds, approximately 4" long. Bend each piece in half. Holding ends, push top down toward center, creating a diamond shape. Do not twist ends together. Repeat 15 times for 16 untwisted diamonds.

2. Fold one untwisted diamond crosswise over another, creating a dimensional diamond. Twist the four ends together and shape. Repeat for eight dimensional diamonds.

3. Cut four 4" lengths from wire. Thread each piece through a metallic bead.

4. Holding bottom end of one beaded wire at bottom of dimensional diamond, run top end of wire up through and over cross-section of diamond, coming back down through bead. Twist wire ends around pipe cleaners at bottom.

5. Center bead in the diamond. A dab of hot glue may be added to secure bead in place. Repeat for four beaded diamonds.

6. Wind a pipe cleaner tightly in a spiral, creating a flat circle. Repeat for two circles. Set one aside.

7. Hot-glue twisted ends of one beaded diamond toward center of first circle.

8. Hot-glue one plain diamond to circle, next to beaded diamond.

9. Evenly space and hot-glue remaining diamonds around the circle, alternating beaded and plain until ornament has been formed.

10. Glue remaining pipe cleaner circle on top of the first, covering all twisted ends.

11. Hang ornament from ornament hanger.

Pearl Heart & Star

- 7mm pearls (102)
- Beads, color and size of choice (3)
- Floss
- Needle-nosed pliers
- Wire, 18-gauge (27")
- Wire cutters

Heart

1. Cut a 9" length from wire. Set remaining aside for Star Ornament.

2. Loop one end of wire length to prevent pearls from falling off.

3. String pearls onto wire, leaving approximately ¼" at the end of wire.

4. Count 16 pearls and bend wire in half. Pull ends of wire out and around to form into shape of heart with looped end at bottom tip. Thread straight end of wire through looped end and fold over. Secure with pliers.

5. Cut 6" length from floss and tie floss ends to top of heart, forming a loop hanger.

Star

1. String beads onto remaining wire, following Steps 2–3 for Heart on opposite page.

2. Form a star shape with seven beads per bend of wire.

3. Cut 10" length from floss. Tie 6" of one end at top of star, forming a 3" loop as a hanger and allowing remaining end to hang down.

4. Thread two beads onto end of floss, positioning at center of star. Tie a knot to secure beads. Repeat for one bead at end of floss.

Sequined Star

- Craft glue
- Craft scissors
- Gray felt, 4½" square
- Gray sewing thread
- Ornament hook
- Sewing machine
- Sewing needle
- Silver braided rope (4")
- Silver sequins
- Transfer paper

1. Enlarge and transfer the *Star Pattern* below. Cut two stars from felt.

2. Place felt stars together and machine-stitch a ¼" seam allowance around star edge, leaving a 1" opening at top of one star point.

3. Loop silver braided rope and hand-stitch ends to opening, creating a hanger. Turn star right side out and hand-stitch opening closed.

4. Apply a dab of craft glue to the back of each sequin and place on star. Repeat to cover entire star. Allow to dry.

5. Attach ornament hook through braided loop to hang.

Star Pattern
Enlarge 135%

Snowy Christmas Village

Create a winter wonderland with these miniature houses. Children's imaginations will light up at the prospect of these tiny dwellings.

Supplies listed are for one house

- Clear acetate sheeting
- Chipboard
- Craft glue
- Craft knife
- Craft scissors
- Crystal glitter, assorted colors
- Foam brushes, ½" (2)
- Lightweight cardboard
- Paper cup
- Pencil
- Permanent markers: green, red, white, yellow
- Ruler
- Scrap paper
- Silver metallic spray paint
- Small bottle-brush trees, color of choice (2)
- White acrylic paint

House Colors

Blue House

- House: aqua blue crystal glitter
- Roof, base, floor mat, chimney trim, door and window trim: white crystal glitter
- Trees: silver metallic

Red House

- House: Red crystal glitter
- Roof, base, floor mat, chimney trim, door and window trim: white crystal glitter
- Trees: silver metallic

White House

- House: white crystal glitter
- Roof, base, and floor mat: white crystal glitter
- Door and window trim: red crystal glitter
- Trees: silver metallic

General House Assembly

1. Enlarge and photocopy **House Patterns** on pages 62–63. Transfer house pieces onto chipboard including framework around doors and windows, and base onto cardboard. Cut out sections with a craft knife. Score on dotted lines.

2. Adhere applicable Frames onto doors and windows. Let dry.

3. Paint all pieces white. Let dry.

4. Working with one section at a time, use a foam brush to apply craft glue to a section. Over a piece of scrap paper, pour crystal glitter from a paper cup over the glued portion. Let sit for one minute. Tap extra glitter onto paper. Roll paper and pour glitter back into cup. Repeat for all pieces.

5. Trace outline of each window onto acetate sheeting. Draw panes inside outline of windows with white permanent marker.

6. Trim acetate windows with scissors, leaving approximately ¼" allowance on all sides. Adhere acetate windows to inside openings of house with craft glue.

7. Spray bottle-brush trees with silver metallic paint. Let dry.

8. Construct house, using craft glue and foam brush. Follow assembly instructions for individual house.

Blue House

1. Fold *House (A)* along scored lines, gluing where right side overlaps onto the back.

2. Fold *Chimney (B)* along scored lines, gluing where right side overlaps onto the back.

3. Glue *Chimney Trim (C)* along top edge of *Chimney (B)*. Glue completed *Chimney (B)* on rear-left side of house, with edge of chimney lined up with house.

4. Fold *Roof (D)* along scored lines and glue onto house, lining up with house edges. Roof will overhang on the house.

5. Place *Platform (E)* on flat surface. Center and glue house on rear edge of *Platform (E)*. Glue *Floor mat (F)* to *Platform (E)*, in front of door.

6. Attach a bottle-brush tree onto each front corner of *Platform (E)* by twisting bottoms into cardboard.

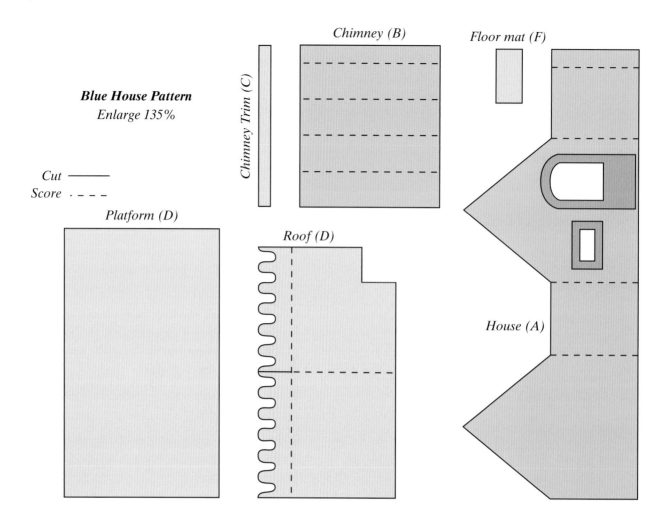

Chimney (B)

Floor mat (F)

Chimney Trim (C)

Blue House Pattern
Enlarge 135%

Cut ———
Score - - - -

Platform (D)

Roof (D)

House (A)

Red House

1. Fold *House (A)* along scored lines, gluing where right side overlaps onto the back.

2. Fold *Chimney (B)* along scored lines, gluing where right side overlaps onto the back.

3. Glue *Chimney Trim (C)* along top of *Chimney (B)*, covering top edge.

4. Fold *Roof (D)* along scored lines, gluing to top of house, lining up with house edges. Roof will overhang on the house.

5. Glue completed *Chimney (B)* to *Roof (D)* with long side lining up with edge of roof.

6. Center and glue house on rear edge of *Platform (E)*.

7. Glue *Floor mat (F)* to *Platform (E)*, placing in front of door.

8. Attach one bottle-brush tree on each front corner of *Platform (E)* by twisting bottoms into cardboard.

White House

1. Fold *House (A)* along scored lines, gluing where right side overlaps onto the back.

2. Fold *Roof (B)* along scored lines, gluing to the top of house, lining up with house edges. Roof will overhang on the house.

3. Center and glue house on rear edge of *Platform (C)*.

4. Glue *Floor mat (D)* to *Platform (C)*, placing in front of door.

5. Attach one bottle-brush tree on each front corner of *Platform (C)* by twisting bottoms into cardboard.

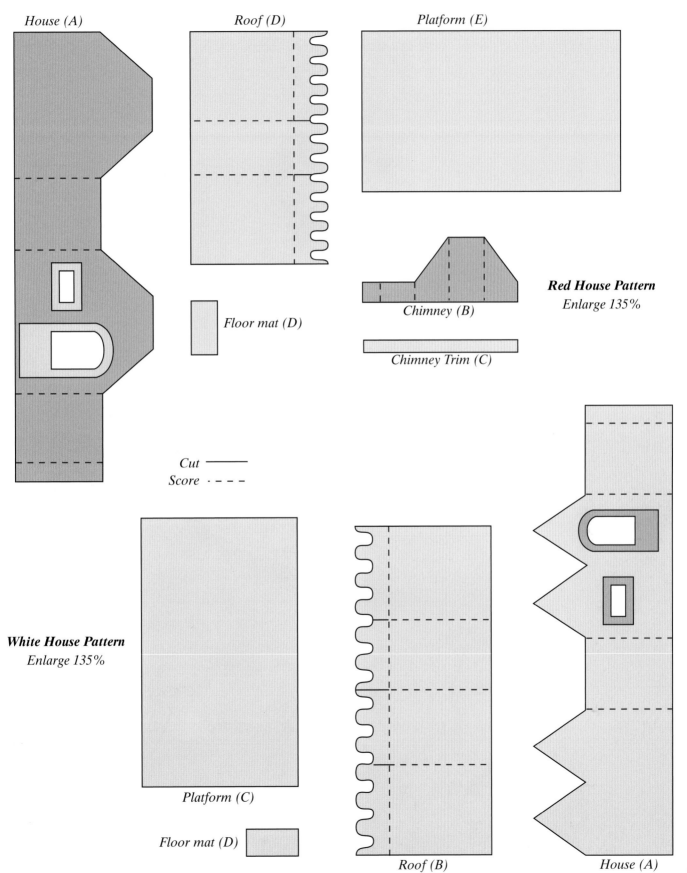

House (A)

Roof (D)

Platform (E)

Floor mat (D)

Chimney (B)

Chimney Trim (C)

Red House Pattern
Enlarge 135%

Cut ——————
Score · - - - -

White House Pattern
Enlarge 135%

Platform (C)

Floor mat (D)

Roof (B)

House (A)

63

Heart of Gold

As an ornament or gift, these hearts are certain to warm the heart when added to the collection of a lucky recipient.

- Assorted buttons and pearls (10–12)
- Assorted purchased ribbon rosettes
- Brass charms (4–6)
- Cream fabric, 3" x 6"
- Cream lace trim, ½" wide (4")
- Dark gold fabric bow, 3"
- Gold fabric, 1¼" x 15"
- Hot-glue gun and glue
- Iron and ironing board
- Lightweight cardboard, 6" square
- Metallic gold braid (½ yard)
- Pencil
- Ribbon rose
- Scissors: craft, fabric
- Silk ribbons, ⅛" wide: light gold, dark gold (½ yard each)
- White fleece, 3" square

1. Enlarge and photocopy the *Heart Pattern* at right. Using inside pattern, transfer and cut two hearts from cardboard and one from fleece. Using outside pattern, cut two hearts from cream fabric.

2. For front, glue fleece heart to one cardboard heart. Center cardboard/fleece piece, fleece-side down, on wrong side of one fabric heart. Wrap edges of cream fabric snugly and glue edges to secure to cardboard side.

3. For back, glue remaining cardboard and fabric hearts together. Wrap and glue edges. Set back aside.

4. Cut one 6" length from gold braid; set remaining aside. Fold length in half, tying a knot 1" from folded end. Glue tails to back side of heart front, forming a hanger.

5. Glue fabric bow to knot of hanger and embellish with charms and ribbon rose.

6. Cut one 12" length each of light and dark gold ribbon. Handling as one, tie a small bow. Attach to top center of heart front. Cascade tails on either side, following

Cascade instructions on page 53. Glue buttons and pearls to tails. Embellish heart front with charms, buttons, pearls, and rosettes as desired.

7. For ruffle, press 1¼" x 15" strip of gold fabric in half lengthwise, matching long edges. Running-stitch thread along raw edges. Gather to fit heart. Beginning at top center of heart, glue ruffle to wrong side of heart front three-quarters around. Glue cream lace around remaining quarter of heart.

8. Center and glue wrong sides of heart front and back together. Wrap and glue remaining gold braid around outside edge.

Heart Pattern
Enlarge 135%

Old Things Not Forgotten

Redefining the old and keeping its timeless appeal is a great aspect of the Chic Vintage Christmas Style. The Christmas season generates nostalgia for the past, memories shared over hot chocolate and homemade marshmallows. At the beginning of the holiday decorating, unwrapping each item brings back these memories. A tree topper from Grandma's house, a favorite ornament from a sister, or a stocking from your childhood are items worth saving.

Embellish Old Things

Instead of placing your collection of miniature decorative bottle-brush trees randomly around the house, group them together to maximize their impact as shown on opposite page. Spread a drop cloth in the basement and spray-paint trees in colors coordinating with your style and theme. Here, soft metallics and flaked snow add to the Chic Vintage feel. Paint the bases white and allow to dry. When dry, brush with a thin coat of clear-drying craft glue, sprinkle vintage mica snow onto the glue, and allow to dry. Hot-glue small ornament balls and wrap various trims around the tree, securing ends with hot glue. Intertwine beaded garlands around the bases, looping it around for a soft flowing feel. Placed on a mantel, baker's rack, or coffee table, this group of trees brings a Chic Vintage forest into the home.

These crystal-beaded spheres at left are especially beautiful to hang in front of windows or glass doors, to capture and reflect the light. Wrap wired clear or crystal beads around simple wire spheres. Loop a wide ribbon through and tie a knot at the top of the sphere. Using more ribbon, tie a double-looped bow at the top of the sphere, trimming ends to desired length.

Designer Displays

Finding new and beautiful uses for old decorations like those below and on page 68, is what Chic Vintage is all about. When unpacking holiday decor, think of something different to use them for, or somewhere new to place them. Changing the placement and giving them a new look makes them appear as if they are new altogether.

Christmas Villages

Nothing brings back memories of past Christmases like seeing vintage Christmas villages. Simple and fun, making them can easily become a holiday tradition. These tiny houses make a strong statement, and their vintage look and classic appeal will look fabulous in any home. They can be decorated to match each

Instead of putting treetop ornaments, shown on the opposite page, on the trees, put them together in a group setting. Their fluted ends should be strong enough to keep them upright; however, just to be safe, you may want to hot-glue the base of the tree topper to a thick piece of cardboard cut to a square, for added balance. Place on a flat surface and cover bases with vintage mica snow.

other, to coordinate with your decorating theme, or done differently to represent the person who made it. Placed on glass cake stands, as shown above, or atop a mantel, this little village will be admired by all. Set these on top of angel hair and sprinkle vintage mica snow over the grouping to create a miniature winter wonderland.

Chic Decorating

Create a formal setting by wiring crystal chandelier drops to glass candleholders. If you don't have drops, make your own by stringing glass or crystal beads onto a thin gauge wire. Use candles and candleholders in various heights and designs. Mix glass and silver candleholders, creating a very chic atmosphere.

The ornaments on the opposite page can be easily made from purchased glass ball ornaments. They are easy to find and so popular that you may just find a box or two of them in the basement or the attic. Many times I have found these at second-hand stores, just waiting for someone to give them new life. A great time to buy these is at the after-Christmas sales. They can be purchased at a bargain and stored away until next season.

Using a marker, draw on designs that you wish to create. With clear-drying craft glue, trace over lines. Immediately cover with glitter, vintage mica snow, ribbons, or other embellishments and let dry. You can also use acrylic paints or draw on them with permanent markers. Attach hand-dyed ribbon or braided cord for a hanger with an extra finishing touch.

Just as the possibilities for design are endless, so are the many ways in which these can be used. Besides your own decor, make in sets and give away as a gift for neighbors and friends. When giving a gift, embellish an ornament, complete with that person's name, and attach with a ribbon for a unique keepsake name tag. When having friends and family over for a Christmas brunch or dinner, decorate an ornament specific to them and their likes. Loop ribbon through and tie to the back of their chair. Not only will your guests know where to sit, they will take a thoughtful favor home with them. In our neighborhood, it is popular to give small gifts; but with all the great neighbors I have, this could become costly. Decorating glass balls is cost effective and unique. This is a truly original and useful gift for the receiver. Given alone, in a set, or tied to a box of homemade goodies, this is a great way to wish them a Merry Christmas.

Elegance in Creamy White

These churches on the opposite page, have lights placed behind the doors, creating a warm and welcoming feel when the lights go down. Store-bought or handmade, the simplistic white-on-white is an elegant Chic Vintage look. If you have plaing wooden or paper churches, brush on a coat of clear-drying craft glue and sprinkle with vintage mica snow and glitter. If your church doesn't have a night-light attached to it, drill a small hole and add one yourself. The serene look is completed with frosted white Christmas trees and a dusting of vintage mica snow on the ground.

The end of summer doesn't have to mean the end of your outside decor. The cherub and urn shown above, were thoroughly cleaned, dried, and brought in for the holiday season. Ornaments are placed in the cherub's bowl and he is surrounded by Chic Vintage items that complement his style. The urn is also filled with simple ornaments, so the focus is on the cherub and his thoughtful watch over the holiday celebration.

Etched Glass Greetings

Etching glass is surprisingly easy and very enjoyable. See page 12 for an etched-vase idea. You are only limited by your imagination.

Note: Etching cream will permanently etch all glazed surfaces immediately. Avoid letting cream touch any area you do not want to etch, including porcelain sinks. Be very careful with the putty knife, so as not to lift any tape before the etching paste is thoroughly removed.

- Assorted jewels
- Black permanent marker, fine tip
- Circle cutter
- Contact paper
- Etching cream
- Glass, size of choice
- Glass cleaner
- Glass glue
- Lint-free paper towels
- Plastic putty knife
- Rubber gloves
- Ruler
- Scissors
- Tape
- Transfer paper

1. Clean glass surface. Dry with lint-free paper towels.

2. The bottom of the glass is done by measuring where to place the stripes with a ruler. Draw a line for tape placement, using permanent marker. Apply different widths of tape to create the stripes on the glass.

3. For the circle behind the jewels, use a circle cutter from a scrapbook supply store. Cut circles the same size as the jewels, out of contact paper. Use a ruler and measure where you want the jewels to be. Using a permanent marker, make a dot and place the sticky contact paper circle over it.

4. Press tape and contact paper designs tightly to adhere so there are no loose edges or air bubbles for the etching cream to get under. Be certain to remove any fingerprints or smudges on the glass after applying tape or etching cream will not etch evenly. *Note: If you apply the markings to reverse side of the glass you do not have to worry about removing the marker before etching glass.*

5. Transfer *Lettering Pattern* below onto contact paper, and cut out. Tape the pattern to back of glass to be etched. Take paper backing off of cut out letters.

6. Using pattern on back of the glass for placement, lay sticky side of lettering in place on glass. Press down tightly with your fingers to remove any air bubbles and to make certain it is securely in place. Wipe any fingerprints from the glass.

7. Pour etching cream on glass and spread, using a plastic putty knife. Let stand for 15 minutes. Using putty knife, scoop excess cream back into bottle to be reused.

8. Using glass cleaner and a paper towel, clean and dry glass. Repeat until all etching cream is removed and glass is clean. Remove paper lettering.

9. Adhere jewels onto nonetched circles with glass glue.

Lettering Pattern
Reduce or enlarge as needed

Jolly Jester

Entertain the fantasy of an adult Christmas. The magic of these jesters is just the beginning to the surprises hiding inside the stocking.

Note: Directions are for one doll. Patterns include ¼" seam allowance.

- Craft glue
- Fabric, color of choice (¼ yard)
- Fabric, contrasting color (¼ yard)
- Fabric scissors
- Gold jingle bell, ⅛" (1)
- Matching thread
- Novelty button, small (1)
- Polymer clay (small package each)
    color choice for head, hands, and feet
    contrasting color for details
- Ribbons: coordinating colors
    ¹⁄₁₆" wide (6")
    1" wide (¼ yard)
- Sewing machine
- Straight pin
- Stuffing

Make Body Pieces

1. Following *Diagram A* below, mold head, hands, and feet from polymer clay. Flatten ends that will extend into clothing. Make cheeks, lips, and desired embellishments from contrasting polymer clay.

Diagram A

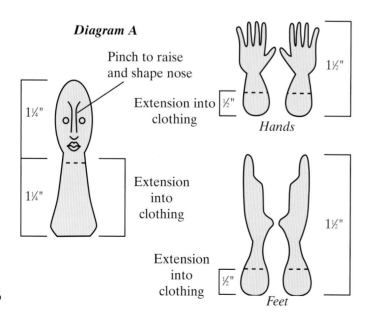

Pinch to raise and shape nose

1¼"

1¼"

Extension into clothing

Extension into clothing

Feet

Extension into clothing

½"

1½"

½"

1½"

Hands

2. Glue cheeks and lips to face. Glue other details as desired. Use straight pin to make slight indentations for eyes, nostrils, and eyebrows.

3. Following manufacturer's instructions, bake or harden body pieces.

Make Clothing

4. Transfer *Jester Patterns* on page 77 onto fabric and cut out.

5. Open each body piece. Place two body pieces together, right sides facing, and sew along *A* edges.

6. To make legs, fold one body piece with right sides facing, aligning *A* seams front and

back. Match *B* edges of each fabric piece to itself and sew continous inseam, pivoting at crotch. Turn body right side out.

7. Fold end of one leg under ¼" and gather-stitch near fold; do not cut thread. Glue one flattened side of foot and insert into leg opening. Pull to gather thread around foot and secure. Repeat with remaining leg and foot.

8. With right sides facing, sew short edges of one arm piece together. Turn are right side out. Repeat with other arm piece.

9. Fold end of one arm under ¼" and gather-stitch near fold; do not cut thread. Glue one flattened side of hand and insert into gathered arm opening. Pull to gather thread around wrist and secure. Repeat with remaining sleeve piece and hand.

10. With right sides facing, fold hat piece in half and stitch long edges together. Turn. Tack jingle bell to tip of hat.

Assemble Body

11. Stuff legs and body lightly. Referring to *Diagram B*, fold top edge on each side of body into a ½"-deep pleat. Slip raw end of one sleeve inside one fold and tack securely. Repeat for other sleeve.

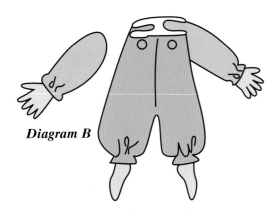

Diagram B

12. Dot one flattened side of neck with glue. Insert neck inside top opening. Let dry overnight.

Complete Ornament

13. Run a gathering thread along one long edge of 1"-wide ribbon. Pull to gather and tie ribbon around neck.

14. Fold raw edge of hat under ¼"; adjust to fit head and glue hat to head.

15. Using photograph on page 76 as a guide, tack button to front of body. Knot ends of ¹⁄₁₆"-wide ribbon together and tack knot at center back of body for hanger.

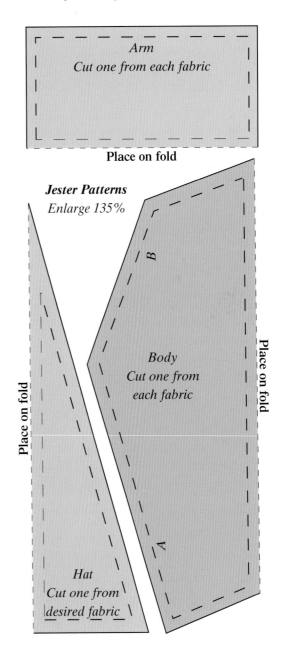

Arm
Cut one from each fabric

Place on fold

Jester Patterns
Enlarge 135%

B

Place on fold

Place on fold

Body
Cut one from each fabric

A

Hat
Cut one from desired fabric

Vintage Christmas Bags

Make gift giving more unique by using these elegant bags as your stockings. Santa is truly stylish this year.

- Butcher paper
- Cord, coordinating color (3½ yards)
- Fabrics: (2⅛ yards each)
  color of choice for outside of bag
  contrasting color for inside of bag
- Fabric scissors
- Iron and ironing board
- Small safety pin
- Sewing machine
- Straight pins
- Tassels, coordinating color(s) (4)

Cutting Materials

1. Using dimensions of **Bag Pattern** at right, draw pattern on butcher paper and cut out.

2. Fold fabric in half lengthwise, selvage edges together. Lay pattern on fabric lengthwise, pin in place, making certain to match plaids or patterns. If using velvet or fabric with a nap, be certain naps are laying the same direction. Cut two pieces for outside. Repeat for inside bags.

Outside of Bag

3. Lay outside pieces with right sides together and sew bottom and side seams. Leave ¾" opening, ½" from top of each side for cord. Press seam allowances open. Turn right side out.

Inside of Bag

4. Lay inside pieces with right sides together and sew bottom and side seams. Leave 4"–6" opening in center of bottom seam. Press seam allowances open. Turn right side out.

Bag Assembly

5. Place outside bag into inside bag, right sides together, matching peaks and side seams.

6. Sew together around top. At top of each peak, leave opening large enough for a small safety pin to pass through. Attach safety pin to loop end of each tassel. At opening in bottom of bag, thread safety pin through to opening at top of each peak. Pull tassel as far to the end as possible. Stitch across each tassel to secure. Remove safety pins.

7. Turn bag right side out by pulling bag through opening in bottom seam. Place inside bag into outside bag.

8. Gently pull each tassel to make certain it is secure.

9. Pin bags together to form casing. Sew inside and outside bags together around the top edge, 1" down from base of peaks.

10. Cut cord into two equal pieces. Pull cord through casing, going in one side opening and coming back out through same opening. Repeat on opposite side.

11. Knot ends of each cord together.

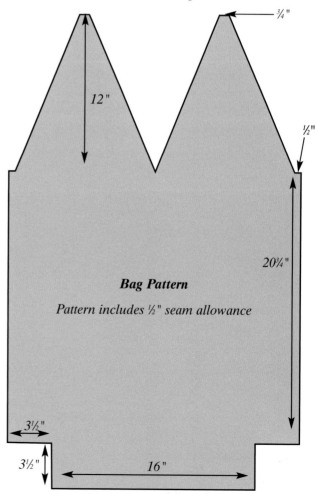

Bag Pattern

Pattern includes ½" seam allowance

¾"

12"

½"

20¾"

3½"

3½"

16"

Your Own Unique Style

I love walking into a store or someone's home and seeing how they have decorated for the Christmas season. Each place is always unique and tailored to their personal style. Every theme is beautiful—there is no right or wrong way. Christmas is about celebrating, so celebrate with style—your own unique style.

Instead of relying on the traditional and safe, decorate how you've always imagined. Do not be afraid to try new and different avenues.

Made Just for You

My mother changes her Christmas theme each year so it is essential that she find ways to make her old ornaments appear to match the current year's theme. She loves copper, silver, gold, white, and crystal. So the majority of what she buys is in these colors. In that way, when she decides on her yearly theme, she can buy a few pieces that are very theme-oriented and put those in the most obvious spots.

The decorations here and on the opposite page are some used when she wanted everything to look like a winter garden. These Christmas trees are topiary forms on which ivy is grown during the summer months. She brought them into the house, removed the ivy, cleaned them, and secured them in metal pots filled with foam and moss. She tied ornaments together in clusters and secured them to the base of the tree spheres. And because my mother is my mother, she added all of her treasures. Look closely and you will see delicate wire bird's nests, hand-dyed satin roses, chandelier crystals, and silver hearts tied among the other ornaments. In my mother's decorating style, you can never have too many ornaments or too many treasures—too much is never enough!

Make a Small Forest

It is often easier to decorate with artificial small trees, but small trees need to be arranged so that they do not appear to be "small." They can be potted in any number of styled pots from Grecian urns to distressed metal buckets, placed on garden pedestals or arranged on a variety of small dressers and trunks. One small tree can be perfect for an apartment and a dozen small trees can be even more special and much more manageable than one large tree for a large home. They are much less daunting because oftentimes smaller trees do not need to be lit and if you do choose to put lights on them, they need fewer than a typical large-sized tree.

Another advantage to smaller trees is that they take fewer ornaments to make them look "very decorated." If you have more than one, there is the option to decorate all the trees the same or do each one differently. This way, all aspects of a theme selected for the holidays can be enjoyed. For example, if you were to choose a Garden Christmas theme, one tree could be decorated with tiny hanging vases filled with water and small fresh flowers, a second tree could be decorated with vintage hand-dyed silk flowers, and a third could be decorated with miniature copper pots filled with tiny potted flowers. If you particularly like one of the trees in this year's theme, use that tree as the holiday theme for next year. This makes it easy to add to your speciality theme when shopping at the after-Christmas sales or flea markets throughout the year.

When decorating with smaller trees, fill in with other items. In the garden theme, pots were brought in from the garden and filled with miniature pine trees. The oversized candleholders were brought in from the back porch and placed among the trees. Garden statuary was used intermittently and a large ornate birdhouse was added at the last minute. Again, more decorations for much less money.

Shabby VINTAGE

A Shabby Vintage Christmas is about using things that are old or look that way. Flea markets, collections, and loving things because they have been "loved and used" is a natural sentimental feeling that comes with the arrival of Christmas. Keepsake ornaments, once confined to an old attic, are given new life when placed amongst other gently used finds. The cracked and worn surfaces give an aged and timeless appeal—one treasured even as colors begin to fade.

Small Spaces

One of our authors, Connie Duran, decorates her studio apartment with small vignettes on every tabletop and in every nook and cranny, displaying each of her treasured antiques and collectibles.

Above and Right: Personal touches, from the hand-sewn tree skirt to the chosen ribbon and gift tag, add flavor and richness and complete the holiday decor.

Never Too Small

When you walk into Connie's apartment, it is a wonderland of hidden delights. I can often spend hours there looking at the vintage Santa Clauses and her miniature trees with their tiny ornaments. Decorating a small space for the holidays can create an inviting and intimate atmosphere. Instead of one large Christmas tree, you could use a few small trees, placed throughout the room. This tinsel tree, shown on the opposite page, is the perfect size to fill in a small space and still display your favorite ornaments. When decorating a tree in a smaller space, make sure you add items around the base of the tree. Filling the floor space with wrapped gifts, vintage snowmen, and holiday dolls adds to the cozy appeal.

Perfectly Wrapped

When decorating for Christmas, the small handmade details can make a tremendous difference. Wrapping your gifts is no exception. If your decorations are a Shabby Vintage Style the wrapping paper, tags, and bows should follow the same theme. Vintage papers, simple brown kraft paper, or old pages torn from books look wonderful with tea-dyed satin ribbons. When you are shopping, be certain to look for wrapping paper and ribbons in your chosen theme. Details like these bring charm and character to your gifts and your holiday decor.

Bottle-brush Christmas Trees

Holiday decor can be displayed anywhere in the home, including a section of your everyday shelves like those shown above. This is a good place to display Christmas plates or other items that may be too fragile to put out in the open.

A great way to add the holiday spirit to any shelf or tabletop is by adding decorated trees. Spray-paint miniature bottle-brush trees in the desired color. The trees above are painted with the bases white and the trees themselves an antique ivory. Pearl beads are hot-glued onto the trees as ornaments. The tone-on-tone coloring is an excellent way to bring in the Shabby Vintage Christmas feel.

Opposite: Mixing Christmas items such as the snowflake tinsel hanging from the mirror and pictures with everyday decorations is an easy way to give a new look to old pieces and use various leftover decorations.

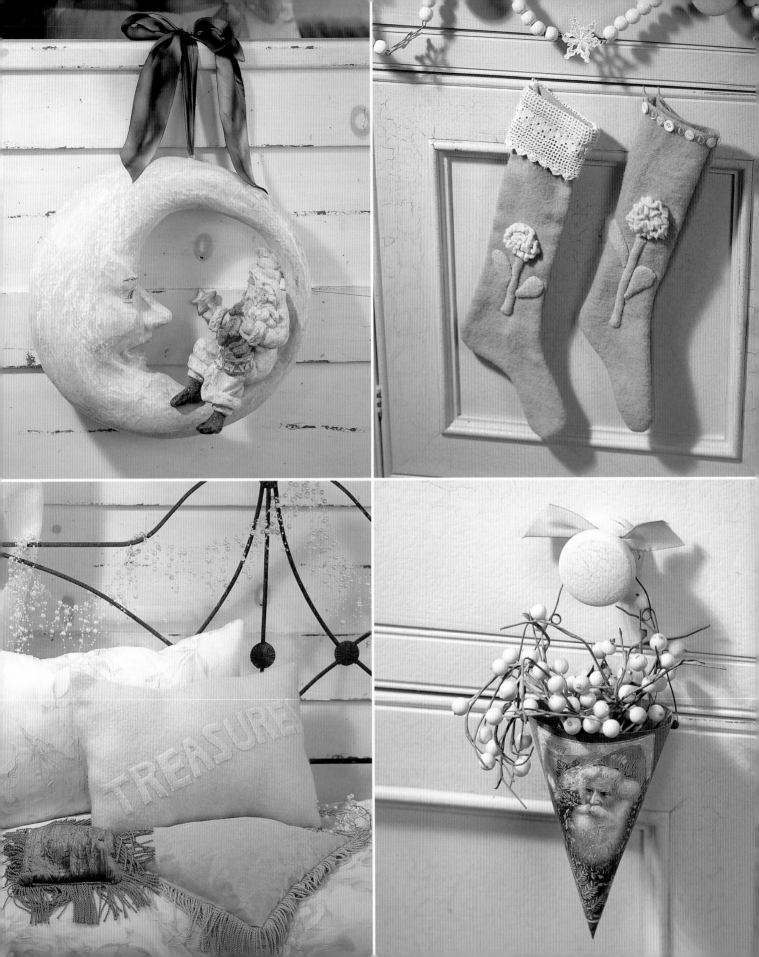

Jolly Holiday Clown

A primitive clown is a magical addition to any Christmas decor, perfect for creating a vintage feel.

- Acrylic paints: black, burgundy, light brown, cream, orange, red
- Antique snow
- Bowl buttons (4)
- Buttons, mini (2)
- Cellophane tape
- Clear glitter
- Cotton swab
- Crackle medium
- Cream/rose ribbon, wire-edged, 1½" wide (18")
- Drill and bits: ³⁄₃₂", ³⁄₁₆"
- Face blush
- Hair dryer
- Hot-glue gun and glue
- Liner paintbrush
- Mint green felt, 12" square
- Mint green water-stained taffeta (⅓ yard)
- Molded craft foam, 5" pear shape
- Newspaper
- Paper stem wire, 18-gauge (2)
- Plastic foam egg, 2½"
- Quilted muslin (⅝ yard)
- Sandpaper
- Scissors: craft, fabric
- Screws, 1⅝" (2)
- Small bird
- Tacky glue
- Toothpicks
- White air-dry modeling clay
- White pom-pom
- Wooden base, 5" x 7"
- Wooden dowel, ⅞" diameter

Shirt

1. Fold muslin in half matching short edges, right sides together. Enlarge and photocopy *Shirt Pattern* on page 94. Cut out shirt.

2. Sew, using ¼" seam allowances. Turn shirt right side out. Cut a 5" horizontal slit in the center of fold for neck opening.

3. Add 2 ounces of burgundy acrylic paint to 8 cups hot water and mix thoroughly in bowl. Place shirt completely in mixture. Remove and wring out excess water. Wash hands.

Continued on page 95

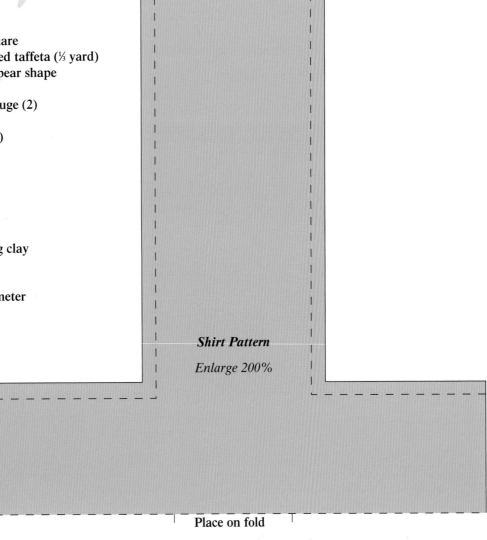

Shirt Pattern

Enlarge 200%

Place on fold

Continued from page 93

4. Use hair dryer to dry shirt completely. Sew two buttons to front, using photograph on page 93 as a guide.

5. Hot-glue 1" hem around shirt bottom. Repeat for each sleeve edge.

Pants

6. Cut two 6" x 12" pieces. With right sides together, sew along the long edges, using ¼" seam allowance. Center and sew two seams 6½" from one short edge to the middle leaving ½" space between seams. Cut 6" between seams. Turn the pants right side out. *See Diagram A below.*

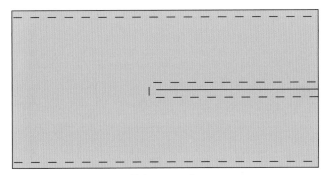

Diagram A

Hat

7. Fold felt in half. Measure 9" along fold and mark. Cut at a diagonal from bottom corner to 9" mark. *See Diagram B.* Sew along cut edge with a ¼" seam allowance. Turn hat right side out. Turn up ½" to form cuff. Hot-glue pom-pom on top

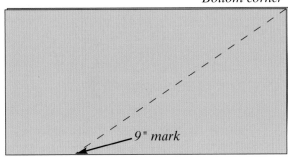
Bottom corner

9" mark

Diagram B

Head

8. Using large pieces of clay, pat out to ⅛" thickness and cover pear shape. Smooth seams together with a wet finger until no lines remain. Continue doing this until entire pear is covered and smooth. Leave bottom tip of pear bare to be glued to the neck. *Note: The point of the pear will be chin and neck.*

9. Place two small pieces on pear shape, forming an eye slit. Smooth out edges. Repeat for other eye. Smooth area between eyes.

10. Roll a small piece of clay into a cone shape for nose. Insert a ¼" piece of toothpick into face where nose will be. Press cone shape onto toothpick. Smooth area around nose. Press a toothpick into clay to form a smile. Let head dry.

11. Paint entire head with cream paint. Using photograph on page 93 as a guide, paint face details with paintbrush. Use cotton swab to apply face blush for cheeks. Glue hat to top of head.

12. With watered-down light brown paint, lightly brush face in random places and in corners of both eyes. Sand tip of nose.

Base

13. Following directions on crackle medium package, paint and crackle wooden base, using light brown and cream paint.

14. Sand randomly around edges to create a worn look. Measure 1" from each side of center and drill a ⅛" hole.

Legs and Body

15. Cut two 7" pieces from dowel.

16. Drill a 3/16" hole through each dowel, ½" from end. On other end, center and drill a 3/32" hole 1" deep into dowel end. Paint dowels with cream paint.

17. Insert wire through 3/16" holes on both dowels, leaving a 1¼" space between dowels and turn both ends of wire up.

18. Roll six pieces of newspaper into a tube about 2" in diameter. Bend in half and crimp at fold to narrow to 1¼" wide. Inset tube below wire between dowels and fold ends up covering wire to form body. *See **Diagram C** below.* Cut tube ends off to 8". Wrap tube and wire with tape, leaving 1" at top unwrapped.

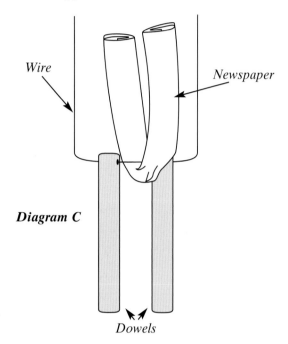

Wire

Newspaper

Diagram C

Dowels

19. Slide on and hot-glue top of pants to body.

20. Insert screw in each hole from underside of base until tips come out at top. Place dowels on screws so that tips of screws are entering holes drilled in dowels. Finish drilling screws from bottom up into dowels until tight against base.

Shoes

21. Roll plastic foam egg on table with palm of hand to make smaller. Cut in half from small end to large end. Cut a "V" shape on the smaller end and press against dowel to make it round. Flatten two pieces of clay and form over egg. Trim off excess. Flatten two pieces of clay to form a 1¼" x 3" strip. Round ends.

22. Curl around legs to form a half circle. Remove and let dry. Paint eggs and strips with light brown paint. Hot-glue eggs to front of dowels and press firmly to base, creating shoes. Hot-glue two buttons on top of each shoe. Sand rounded top of shoes lightly.

Arms

23. Roll two pieces of clay into two ¾" x 8" tubes. Work these clay tubes over both ends of a paper stem wire. Smooth seams together with a wet finger until no lines remain.

24. Place center of wire (with no clay) into middle of newspaper body and hot-glue into place. Bend arms into shape, making certain to form a flat hand on one arm to hold bird. Let dry. Paint arms with cream acrylic paint. Put shirt on body being careful with arms.

25. Push edges of sleeves up to desired length and hot-glue in place.

26. Hot-glue head onto newspaper tilting it slightly. Hot-glue top of shirt together by pinching around neck.

27. Run a gathering stitch along one edge of wired-edged ribbon. Gather to fit neck.

28. Turn up hem at bottom of pants. Pull a pleat on front of each leg and tack in place. Push pant legs up to desired height and glue securely in place.

29. Paint bird with several coats of cream paint, drying between each coat. Water down light brown paint and lightly paint bird.

30. Dot eyes with black paint.

31. Rub patches of glue on bird with a cotton swab. Sprinkle over glue with glitter, shaking off excess. Glue bird to hand.

32. Lightly "scruff" watered-down light brown paint randomly on pants, top, hat, pom-pom, exposed legs, and arms.

33. Using a cotton swab, apply tacky glue randomly on shoes, pants, top, hat, and pom-pom. Apply glitter and antique snow. Shake off excess.

Embellish What You Have

When Connie decorates for the holidays, items that are enjoyed all year play a major part in her holiday decor. It appears that she has more decorations than there really are and makes her holiday decorating easier to set up and take down. For example, the cats at right were found at an antique show in Boulder, Colorado. They are weighted doorstops that are used in several rooms throughout the spring and summer to help hold the doors open. During the holidays, she moves them to a shelf in the kitchen and surrounds them with tiny bottle-brush trees, and sometimes even hangs tiny white berry wreaths around their necks.

Christmas decorations in unexpected places are an added surprise. Everyone expects stockings and garlands on the fireplace, Christmas trees in the living or family room, and a wreath on the front door. Why not hang your stockings from someplace new, hang a wreath on the bathroom door in addition to the front door, and put a small tree on the back patio or in the kitchen.

Another designer trick to make your holiday dollars go further is to redesign some much-used items from year to year, such as the Christmas stockings shown at lower right. Connie only changes the cuff on the stockings each year. This year she photo-transferred images from her granddaughter's favorite book onto tea-dyed muslin and then added the cuffs to her home-spun red stockings. Some years, she has embroidered cuffs with names and one year the cuffs were made from bits and pieces of old lace. Such small additions make the holidays simpler but do not sacrifice the opportunity to be creative. It just takes a few minutes to make a new cuff each year; but it can take weeks to make new stockings once all the decisions are made, such as what material to use, what the cuff design will be, what the theme should be this year. Doing just a new cuff quickly answers all the questions and solves the problems easily.

Sweet Angel

The can to the left is actually used as a vase for fresh flowers on the patio during the summer. For the holidays, it is filled with a variety of other Christmas items, a favorite Christmas ornament is hung from the side, and it is set under the tree in place of packages.

- Acrylic paints: light brown, gold
- Antique snow
- Bowl
- Cheesecloth, thick, 11" x 6"
- Cotton swabs
- Cream ribbon, sheer, ¼" wide (20")
- Faux fur, 4" x 1½"
- Feather wings, 3½" (2)
- Fine-grit sandpaper
- Hot-glue gun and glue
- Ivory ribbing, 1½" wide (4")
- Maroon flannel, 5" circle
- Muslin, 11" x 2½"
- Paintbrush
- Hand-sewing needle
- Paper stem wire, 5"
- Polyester stuffing
- Porcelain angel head and hands, 1½"
- Scissors
- Sewing machine
- Tacky glue
- Tea bag
- Threads, coordinating colors
- White glitter
- Wire, 20-gauge
- Wire cutters
- Wire-edged lace trim, 4" wide (6")

Dress and Cape

1. Pour two cups hot water into bowl over tea bag. Soak for one minute, remove and squeeze excess water from tea bag.

2. Place cheesecloth, faux fur, and lace trim in brewed tea. Soak for one minute, remove and squeeze out excess tea. Dry thoroughly.

3. Fold cheesecloth in half. Machine-sew along 6" edges, using a ¼" seam allowance. Sew a ½" deep hem around bottom edge, leaving 1" opening next to the seam.

4. Cut 12" length from 20-gauge wire. Loop one end of wire and thread around hem, starting and ending at the 1" opening.

5. Loop remaining end through beginning wire loop. Crimp closed. Hand-stitch the 1" opening closed.

6. Hand-stitch a gathering stitch along top edge. Do not gather yet.

7. Using flannel, repeat Steps 3–6 above for cape.

Hat

8. With right sides together, pin long edge of faux fur to long edge of ribbing. Sew together, using a ¼" seam allowance. Fold fur-trimmed ribbing in half and sew together on 1½" side, using ¼" seam allowance.

9. Sew a gathering stitch along one long edge of ribbing, pulling thread tightly to close. Knot and cut thread. Turn remaining edge up ½" to expose fur side and hand-stitch in place.

Body

10. Fold muslin in half. Beginning at cut end, sew along one 5½" edge, using a ¼" seam allowance. Refer to *Diagram 1*. Round at fold to form leg, then sew 2½" up center. Leave ½" between the center seams. Sew back down, rounding the fold, then along remaining side.

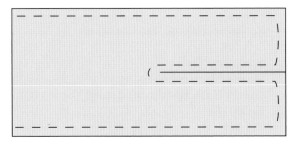

Diagram 1

11. Trim off excess fabric around both feet and cut between legs. Turn body right side out.

12. Cut two 6" pieces from 20-gauge wire and bend in half, forming a U shape. Insert each bent end into legs.

13. Stuff body lightly with stuffing.

14. Hot-glue one hand to each end of a paper stem wire.

15. Sew a gathering stitch along top edge of body. Cut a small slit on each side of body ¼" down. Slide arms through slits. Glue in place. Pull the gathering stitch so it fits tightly around angel-head neck. Knot and cut thread.

16. Slip dress and lace over legs up to arms, pulling thread ends tightly and knotting.

17. Cut 12" from sheer ribbon and tie a bow under arms, over lace.

18. Sew a gathering stitch around hole in flannel. Slip over head and pull tightly under chin, creating a cape.

19. Spread over arms and pinch wire, creating a ruffled look.

20. Hot-glue hat onto head.

21. Paint shoes on feet with gold acrylic paint.

22. Scrunch up edges of dress and lace, making certain to show off feet.

23. Load paintbrush with watered-down light brown acrylic paint. Randomly paint on dress, legs, lace, hat, and feather wings.

24. Fold remaining sheer ribbon in half. Hot-glue ends to back of body, leaving a loop above head for hanger.

25. Hot-glue wings to back of body covering ends of hanger.

26. With a cotton swab, apply tacky glue anywhere you want glitter and antique snow. Apply glitter and antique snow. Shake off excess.

27. Lightly sand cheeks and nose with sandpaper.

Stocking Ornament

A perfectly vintage ornament for any home and decor.

- Acrylic paints: light brown, rose, antique white
- Clear glitter
- Cotton swab
- Crackle medium
- Cream ribbon, sheer, ¼" wide (6")
- Hot-glue gun and glue
- Needled-cotton quilt batting, 12" square
- Paintbrush, #12
- Paper roses, small (3)
- Polyester stuffing
- Scissors
- Sewing machine
- Sticker of choice
- Tacky glue
- Thread, coordinating color
- Tracing paper
- Watercolor paper, 2" square
- White pipe cleaner

1. Fold quilt batting in half. Trace *Stocking Pattern* on page 102 and cut out two from batting.

2. Sew pieces together, using a ¼" seam allowance, leaving top open. Clip edges and turn right side out. Roll top down twice to form cuff.

3. Using paintbrush, paint entire stocking with antique white. Allow to dry thoroughly.

4. Lightly stuff stocking. Scrunch stocking in hands to form creases.

5. Dilute a small amount of light brown paint to an inky consistency. Load paintbrush and scruff over stocking to make random dark patches. Allow to dry thoroughly. *Note: It is better to do light coats instead of heavy ones.*

6. Cut watercolor paper in an oval to fit the sticker. Paint one side with light brown. Let dry. Paint over light brown with one coat crackle medium and let dry thoroughly. Being careful not to overstroke, paint over crackle medium with one coat antique white. Let dry. Adhere sticker to painted oval.

7. Hot-glue pipe cleaner around edges of oval. Scruff pipe cleaner with antique white.

8. Load paintbrush with watered-down light brown paint and lightly dab onto sticker, pipe cleaner, and paper roses.

9. Water down rose paint and dab on edges of paper roses.

10. Hot-glue completed sticker onto stocking, placing near top.

11. Apply a small amount of tacky glue on a cotton swab and rub on stocking randomly where glitter will go. Sprinkle glitter over stocking and shake off excess.

Star Ornament

Add this ornament to a garland or set on the treetop.

- Acrylic paints: light brown, rose, cream, antique white
- Antique snow
- Buttons, neutral colors (10)
- Clear glitter
- Cotton swab
- Crackle medium
- Craft glue
- Doily, 3" round
- Linen thread
- Paintbrushes
- Papier-mâché star, 4½"
- Paper roses (3)
- Pencil
- Polyester stuffing, small amount
- Scissors
- Sewing needle
- Sheer ribbon, coordinating color, ¼" wide (12")
- Sheer ribbon, coordinating color, ½" wide (12")
- Tacky glue
- Tea bag

1. Fold quilt batting in half. Trace papier-mâché star on batting and cut out two stars.

2. Paint bottom and sides of star with light brown paint. Let dry. Paint one heavy coat of crackle medium over light brown paint. Let dry.

Continued on page 102

Stocking Pattern
Shown Actual size

Continued from page 100

3. Paint a heavy coat of cream over crackle medium being careful not to overstroke. Let dry.

4. With needle and linen thread, whipstitch two fabric stars together, leaving bottom edge open. Do not cut thread. Stuff star through open bottom until lightly rounded. Whipstitch bottom edge closed. Knot and cut thread.

5. Glue completed fabric star to unpainted side of papier-mâché star.

6. Paint doily with antique white. Let dry.

7. Soak tea bag in bowl of hot water for a few minutes. Remove tea bag, squeezing out excess water. Dab tea bag all over the fabric star. Let dry.

8. Water down light brown paint. Load brush and lightly scruff all over star and doily. Dab all over buttons and paper roses.

9. Center and glue doily to star. Do not glue down edges.

10. Form a strand by threading buttons through two button holes on linen thread. Bunch buttons together to form an irregular circle. Glue buttons to center of doily.

11. Lightly paint tips of paper roses with watered-down rose paint. Glue roses to doily around outer edges of buttons.

12. Loosely weave ¼"-wide ribbon in and out of edges of doily, gluing randomly to underside of buttons.

13. Apply craft glue with cotton swab to areas that will have glitter and antique snow. Sprinkle glitter and antique snow over glue, tap off excess.

14. Fold ½"-wide ribbon in half and glue to top, creating hanger.

Sculpted Cherub

Add an old-world feel to Christmas with this sweet Cherub.

- Acrylic paints: medium aqua, dark brown, gray
- Antiquing gel
- Cake decorating disposable bag with coupler
- Cake decorating tip #61
- Crackle medium
- Craft glue
- Joint compound, all-purpose (1 qt.)
- Oven
- Paintbrushes: ½" flat, foam, small round
- Plaster cherub, 3½" x 5"
- Plywood tile, ¾" x 8½" square
- Spatula
- Spray matte acrylic sealer

1. Preheat oven to 190°F.

2. Glue cherub to plywood tile, using photograph at right as a guide.

3. Using a spatula and fingertips, apply joint compound to entire board and part of cherub. Fill cake decorating bag half full with joint compound.

4. Practice designs on a piece of foil until comfortable with the process. First make "C" shapes, then add leaves and dots. Next, make the flower petals, and centers.

5. To speed-dry and cause crackling, place tiles in oven for 20 minutes, or until almost dry.

6. Randomly dab dark brown paint onto tile and cherub with small round brush. Let dry.

7. Using foam brush, apply crackle medium, following manufacturer's instructions, over painted areas. Let dry.

8. Mix one tablespoon gray paint with one drop medium aqua paint. Paint tiles with flat brush, allowing crackled areas to show through. Dilute paint with water and use round paintbrush to fill in the small cracks and crevices.

9. Dilute antiquing gel and lightly wash over tiles with flat brush.

10. Spray tiles with matte acrylic sealer. Let dry.

Unexpected Surprises

When decorating for the holidays, use your ornaments in unexpected ways. Your family and friends will expect you to hang them on the tree, adorn a garland, or add them to a wreath. But why not use them in a mantel display where your grandmother's champagne glasses hold your favorite ornaments, shown below left, and add a mirrored tray underneath for a centerpiece.

a stencil and glitter paint, or draw a snowflake with white glue and sprinkle glitter over the design. Let dry.

Tabletop Trees

Tabletop trees are a perfect place to hang small collectible children's toys or delicate porcelain figurines. Use the pieces that may be too small and delicate to hang on the tree, but too important not to have a place of honor.

Create your own vintage snowflake ornament like the one shown above right, by hand-painting a glass ball ornament. Remove the cap and insert a straw, wrapping masking tape around the straw and neck of the ball. Insert the end of the straw into a foam brick to free hands while working. Paint the ball ivory and the cap a darkened gray. Allow to dry thoroughly. Add snowflakes by using

Each year as we were growing up, my mother gave my brother and I a silver ornament with the year engraved on it. They are smaller than my other ornaments and become lost on our big tree, but my small tabletop trees are perfect. Every Christmas my husband and I hang the memories which mean so much to me.

Dress Up Everyday Displays

Vintage plate racks like the one on the opposite page, are a wonderful addition to a decorating scheme anytime of the year. During the Christmas holidays, they are the perfect spot for a small holiday vignette. Here is the place to display vintage Christmas dishes that are too fragile to serve dinner on, but which you want to share. In place of Christmas dishes, display your favorite old books filled with Yuletide stories and recipes. Layer the bottom of the rack with freshly cut pine boughs, add wide cream candles and dried cranberry garland, or drape delicate beaded garlands or hang special ornaments from the rungs. A petite tree decorated with miniature ornaments and garland completes the vignette and can be easily changed throughout the season to showcase a wide variety of decorations as shown on opposite page and above left.

Personalized Gift Tags

What better way to personalize a gift to someone than adding a handmade gift tag to the package like the one above right. Store-bought and mass-produced tags are easy to use, but they are not a very sentimental touch. Make your own by using a sheet of creamy cardstock and cutting out a tag. Cut out a triangle from another piece of cream-colored cardstock to be used as a tree, slightly narrower than the tag. Tea-dye both the tag and the tree to add age to them for a perfect touch to a Shabby Vintage Christmas. Soak a tea bag in a bowl of hot water for a few minutes. When water begins to color, remove tea bag and squeeze out excess water. Lightly sponge tag and tree with it, covering some places heavier than others and allowing to dry thoroughly. Wrap embroidery floss around the tree as garland. Adhere the ends on the back of the triangle with a dab of glue. Glue buttons or other trims to the tree for the ornaments. Glue the tree to the tag, with the tip of the tree almost at the top of the tag. With rubber stamps, stamp the gift recipient's name on the lower part of the tag, under the Christmas tree. Wrap ribbon around tag in a random manner, adhering the ends to the back of the tag with glue. Punch a hole in the top of the tag and loop ribbon through. Tie the tag onto a gift with other ribbons. The recipient will not only enjoy the gift, but the tag as well.

Christmas Memories Collage

Create a collage of favorite holiday memories for displaying and reminiscing.

- Assorted collage items
- Black ink pad
- Craft scissors
- Glue stick
- Hot-glue gun and glue
- Large shipping tag
- Metal-rimmed circular tags, 1½"
- Picture frame with backing, 8" x10"
- Ribbon, ¼" wide (1½" for each circular tag)
- Ribbon, ¾" wide (9½")
- Rubber stamp alphabet
- Scrapbook paper
- Tea, strongly brewed
- Vintage postcards and pictures, photocopied onto cardstock
- Watercolor paintbrush

1. Trim scrapbook paper to fit frame.

2. Paint shipping label and tags with tea until desired shade is achieved. Let dry. This step may need to be repeated. *Note: Prestained tags are available at scrapbook outlets.*

3. Stamp one letter on each metal-rimmed tag and a saying of choice on the shipping label.

4. Arrange postcard and other assorted collage items on trimmed paper. Adhere each item to paper with glue stick.

5. Knot ¼" x 1½" ribbon through metal-rimmed tags as shown.

6. Hot-glue circular tags to collage piece.

7. Tie bow in ¾" x 9½" ribbon and hot-glue to collage piece. Secure ends to back of paper.

8. Frame without glass.

Victorian VINTAGE

"All of the trimmings" is what comes to mind when I think of a Victorian Vintage Christmas. Presents wrapped in the finest of paper with exquisite ribbons and trims adorning them, and Christmas trees laden with beautiful ornaments, with not much room to spare. Awe-inspiring design, the finest of detail—all brought together for this glorious holiday season.

Ornate Settings

An afternoon tea in front of a magnificently decorated tree is saturated with Victorian sensibility. Candles cast a gilded glow over a very civilized and ornate celebration. Dust off your very best manners and indulge in a most traditional and well-loved social engagement.

Above and Opposite: Over-the-top attention to detail extends from the tea set and posy holder to the tree's decor. No detail is too small for a bit of ornate gilding or floral embellishment.

Popcorn Cones

If you love very elegant and beautiful things, decorating your home with a Victorian Vintage theme for Christmas can be a tradition that is cherished more than any other. As they did in times when life was more genteel and ladies had time to spend with friends, this is a holiday decor that begs for afternoon teas and ladies' luncheons. This is a holiday celebration where hand-carameled popcorn is served not in bowls but in vintage papers rolled into cones. Roll a sheet of decorative Christmas paper, bottom corner to opposite top corner, forming a cone shape as you go. Secure edges with tape or craft glue. These cones make wonderful party favors to send special treats home with your guests. Fill them with snacks, a sprig of holiday greenery, and a simple ornament with the date hand-lettered on it. Place the filled cones in a deep bowl and use as a tabletop decoration, ready for guests to take home. This will be a beautiful remembrance of a lovely time spent with you.

Embellished Glassware

Elegant glassware is often expensive to buy but can be easy and affordable to make like the candleholder shown at left. Choose a hurricane-style candleholder and hot-glue a lavish fabric trim around the top. Gold-leaf the base, using supplies available at most craft stores. Once the base is covered, age the gold leaf, using dark brown acrylic paint and a soft towel. Dip the towel in a small amount of paint and working quickly, wipe the base just enough to add definition to the cracks in the gold leaf and mellow the shine. Finish with a coat of satin-finish polyurethane on the gold leaf and allow to dry.

Use creativity to adapt these ideas to an existing holiday theme. The same gold-leafing supplies can be used to embellish simple papier-mâché fruits, plain ornaments, or other items.

Paper Cutting

Handmade decorations are an essential part of a Victorian celebration. Such pieces are usually expensive to purchase but time consuming to make. The scherenschnitte picture on the opposite page, can be a labor of love to cut by hand, or simply a purchased laser-cut design that you have framed. There are many books available with patterns of scherenschnitte designs or do your children's silhouettes, using the same technique they teach in grade school. Tape a piece of paper to the wall and turn out the lights. Stand your subject in front of the paper and project their shadow onto it using a light source such as a flashlight. Trace the silhouette and cut out. Reduce the image to the correct size using any paper that is lightweight enough to cut, yet heavy enough that it will not tear if parts of the design are very intricate, then cut out the image. To frame the piece, purchase an inexpensive frame and paint and embellish as desired. Cut a mat and draw gold lines around it for accent. Mount image on the mat and insert it into the frame.

Left: Gild gifts by simply adding rich golden bows.

Mirror Antiquing

A beautifully aged mirror adds a sense of history and romance as it reflects the flickering holiday candlelight. If you are not fortunate enough to own a treasure such as this, our designer, Elizabeth DuVal author of *Mosaics: Beyond the Basics*, will teach you how to make one.

- Black acrylic paint
- Craft paper
- Chip paintbrushes, assorted sizes
- Latex gloves
- Mask
- Measuring cups
- Metallic powders: gold, silver
- Mirror
- Muratic acid
- Paint stripper
- Scraper
- Sizing
- Soft towel
- Water

1. Turn mirror face down on craft paper and apply paint stripper to mirror back, following manufacturer's instructions, to remove the protective coating. Rinse with clean water. Let dry.

Continued on page 118

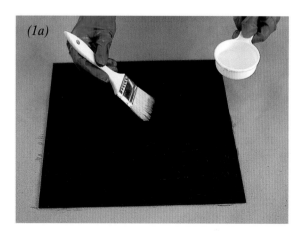

Continued from page 116

2. Use chip paintbrush to spatter muratic acid over approximately two-thirds of mirror surface. Once black spots and silvering deterioration begin to appear, you should be able to see through the glass to the craft paper underneath. Submerge entire piece of glass in clean water to neutralize acid.

(2)

3. Dry back of mirror, using a soft towel. Mix water with black paint in a 1:1 ratio. Use a wet chip brush to spatter spots randomly over entire surface. Let dry.

(3)

4. Apply sizing over entire surface. Allow to sit for approximately 15 minutes.

(4)

5. Wear a mask when working with metal powders. Apply silver powder by dipping a clean, dry brush into pot and tapping it above the surface. Avoid touching mirror with brush because you will get sizing on the brush, which will cause the powder to stick to the brush instead of the mirror. Do not cover entire surface with silver.

(5)

6. Repeat Step 5 above with gold powder. Fill in blank areas to cover entire surface.

(6)

7. Using a clean dry brush, softly brush over entire surface. This will spread the powder and ensure full adhesion.

8. The amount of the gold or silver powder used is up to you. If you want a more silvery look, apply more silver. If you want a more gold look, apply more gold.

Mirror Installation

- Clear silicone adhesive
- Frame
- Latex gloves
- Mirror
- Paper toweling

1. Place frame face down on a flat surface. Insert mirror, face down.

2. Apply clear silicone in space between mirror edge and frame.

3. With a gloved finger, press silicone into the crevice and remove any excess with paper toweling.

4. Silicone will be white when wet, but as it dries it will become clear. Allow to sit undisturbed for 12–24 hours.

5. Once silicone is dry, mirror should be very secure. However, you may still want to apply a paper backing or thin piece of wood to protect the back of the mirror from being scratched.

Candlelit Christmas

A candlelit Christmas is warm, elegant, and breathtaking. Seeing a lighted candle always seems to bring tender feelings of peace and warmth. There is something about a group of glowing candles that draws you into them, their flickering flames beckoning you nearer. Candles can hold many meanings, especially at Christmastime. Whether to remember a special person, time, or event, candles have a way of speaking to our hearts.

Candlesticks

There is nothing more beautiful during the holidays than candles aglow. I bring the candleholders together from every room in my house and cluster them in one spot for my holiday parties like those shown on the opposite page. It has become a tradition for family and friends to give me a new candleholder each year to add to my collection.

Candleholders can be found anywhere, either inexpensive or very costly. A simple way to add numerous candles to your home is to purchase inexpensive holders and dress them up. You can always repaint them to appear as silver or brass; hot-glue pearls, crystal beads, or chandelier drops around the edges; or tie lush bows at the base. Another idea is to buy tall candleholders like those at left, and decorate the surrounding area beneath with objects. Pine boughs, fresh or silk, with hollyberry sprigs and ribbon added are an easy way to create an elegant look with everyday items. Arrange the candles in varying heights, adding dimension to the space.

Candles do present a fire hazard so avoid using them where they might be knocked over. Do not set anything under them that is flammable such as ribbons and greenery, and never leave burning candles unattended.

Out-of-the-Ordinary Centerpieces

Create a unique centerpiece by making this bowl of apples and candles. Simply core out the apples and sprinkle the inside with lemon juice. Insert the stems of silk leaves into the apple and secure them by fitting a candle cup over leaves inside the apple. Place the candle into the cup. Fill the bowl with apples and sprigs of leaves and berries, then place the candle-filled apples on top. The same idea can be adapted as shown on the opposite page using foam balls covered with vintage mica snow instead of apples.

Pinecones and acorns are abundant during the holiday season. Decorate them and use as ornaments, in garlands, or to fill baskets. For another unusual centerpiece, set a silver tray with candles, a teapot, or other items for height. Fill a silver bowl with smaller pinecones and acorns and place in the center of the tray. Place larger pinecones and acorns all around the tray, filling in the remaining empty space and add berries for a hint of color.

Simply VINTAGE

Learning to keep things simple was a lesson that came quickly for Debbie Dusenberry. She worked for many years as a photo stylist in advertising, videos, and motion pictures before opening her store, *The Curious Sofa* in Kansas City. Her style of holiday decorating brings a note of tranquility to a rather hurried, even hectic, season. A soothing palette of creamy whites, sepia, and milk-chocolate browns is an ideal background for focusing the spotlight on decorations that have acquired an aged appeal. It enables her quirky sense of humor to be employed in the arrangement and display of favored pieces. Less is more and the unexpected is truly at home here.

A Champagne Christmas

A pleasing, neutral theme is perfect for quirky displays. From something as unusual as a champagne bottle lamp with an elaborately trimmed shade to a tree skirt made from the newspaper's want-ads, decorations are offbeat and convey a lighthearted attitude and desire not to do anything too traditional.

Glowing Ambiance

This giant antique champagne bottle shown at left, sat for nearly a year before a perfect shade was found for it. What better way to use it than as a lamp to cast an intimate glow over a New Year's Eve celebration for two. Make a lamp out of a favorite bottle using a lamp kit available at a home supply or craft store. Purchase a base approximately ¾" larger around than the base of the bottle. Stain or paint the base a color that will coordinate with the bottle. Using a ½" bit, drill a hole in the center of the base. With a ½" glass drill bit, drill another hole in the center of the bottom of the bottle. Follow the manufacturer's instructions to wire the lamp. Choose a lamp shade that is proportional to the lamp and complements the size and shape of the bottle. The height of the shade should be long enough to cover the light bulb and socket when viewed at eye level.

Opposite: The gray color of a driftwood table sets the tone for a collection of silver objects. Distressed vintage mirrors reflect a beaded tree sprinkled with antique mercury ornaments. A circle cut from a newspaper and pleated is a make-shift tree skirt.

Aged Paper Decor

The holiday decorations featured in the living room above start with an old 1910 newspaper journal found during an antiquing trip. The journal's pages are cut into strips with scalloped edges and hung as a border on the mantel. Pages are also decoupaged onto the hearth's top on the opposite page below left, and offer a unique treatment for an often unattractive surface. Be certain to cover the hearth with several coats of clear acrylic sealer.

The paper theme carries over to a large galvanized star covered with vintage sheet music. Hang the star from an antique mirror to give it pride-of-place above the mantel. The dining table is a fabulous old zinc-topped table with tiny French garden pots that make perfect candleholders arranged down the center of the table.

New alphabet disks shown opposite above left were stained to spell out a seasonal message and hung from a creamy ribbon. Opposite above right, add new battery inserts to a collection of old clocks to bring them back to life or simply set the hands to display your favorite time of day or the party's time. The chair covers, opposite below right, are a simple touch. The pocket could hold a small gift or other conversation-starter to add a unique flair to a dinner party.

Nontraditional Decor

In place of a traditional tree, a wall in the living room shown opposite is decorated to be the centerpiece of the holiday celebration. An old folding screen, covered in Christmas advertisements from an old newspaper journal acts as a backdrop for an antique dressmaker's form. Fabric fringe is hung about the form as a garland, nosegay cones are filled with dusty bottles, photographs, and tiny brush trees. Glittered letters spell out a whimsical theme and an old trombone hangs as a necklace.

The vignette is lit by two simple clip-on lamps shown opposite and below, that can be purchased at a hardware store, They have their own vintage flavor with old correspondence and sheet music decoupaged onto the shade. A worn vintage flower hangs from the base of the shade.

Packages on the floor are wrapped in found materials. Paper nosegay cones made from sheet music covers, above, replace the traditional Christmas stocking. Fill the cones with old photographs, small bottle-brush trees, glitter stars, and dusty bottles to thrill a collector; or personalize with items for individual family members or friends. This idea can be adapted to any gift recipient and any style of Christmas decor simply by using paper and gift items that apply. Give a young child a cone made from whimsical wrapping paper laminated onto cardstock and filled with simple toys such as a jump rope, jacks, small race cars, or farm animal figures. In all of the cones, hide a special something in the tip.

Vintage Adornments

Wrapped packages on the opposite page are made from everyday household papers and carry the theme of a Simply Vintage Christmas to gift giving. Ordinary kraft paper, dressmaker's patterns, maps, ledger paper, and newsprint are cut, torn, and folded in unusual ways. Vintage ribbons, trim, and old hat pins personalize each package. The trims can be selected to hint at what the package contains, or be another small gift on their own.

The neutral pillows, shown below left, were made using a stash of tattered ticking and quilts and adorned with pearl buttons and old lace. They look fabulous tossed on a pair of bergerè chairs that were purchased at an auction and recovered. The ivory pillow was made from the matelassé-like back side of an old quilt whose front pattern had frayed away.

Use the salvageable parts of an old ivory wool blanket to create a new holiday stocking in soothing tones like the one below right. Antique millinery flowers and embroidered lace are classic embellishments in true vintage style. Choose the adornments to reflect the personality of the stocking owner.

Embellished Lamp Shade

Fashion a beautiful lampshade for a flea-market find and create a unique gift.

- Clothespins
- Coffee, strongly brewed
- Craft glue
- Embroidered applique
- Lace collar or lace trim
- Lamp base with shade
- Old paper items:
    sheet music, letters, newspapers
- Paper doilies
- Parchment shade
- Rhinestone button
- Scissors: fabric, craft
- Paintbrush, small

1. Lay out all materials to use and "age" lace and paper items that are too white. Test a hidden spot for color. Lightly apply coffee to items. Let dry between applications to test darkness. Let dry completely.

2. Cut paper to fit around lamp shade and glue in place.

3. Cut and glue small lace trim to top of lamp shade. Leave ⅛" from the edge to avoid the lightbulb.

4. Before gluing, position lace and doilies to see what will fit the lamp shade and looks best. Make note of what needs to be applied first. Cut pleated doilies in half.

5. Work from bottom up. A collar may fit perfectly at bottom, or use collar at top of shade. If a collar is not available, use any lace trim. Fold over and raise in front center to create a scallop. Add lightbulb to lamp and clip shade in place for an easier work surface. Use white glue to adhere all paper and fabric items to shade. Let dry.

6. Hot-glue floral or embroidered embellishment to center of round doily. Glue button to scalloped edge.

Above: This elephant lamp was found at a tag sale and transformed for a Christmas gift. The rewired lamp was topped off with an ordinary parchment shade embellished with a beautiful antique lace collar. Fan-pleated doilies fit perfectly at the base of the lamp.

Opposite: A touch of Christmas in unexpected places such as this bedroom becomes a private celebration for a guest or family member. The chandelier is adorned with a pearl-button garland, metal stars, and glass flowers. Instructions for the garland are on page 136.

candle cover was wrapped with vintage paper and trimmed with old lace. Clusters of metal and glass stars and leaves were taken apart and hung separately around the chandelier.

Buttons strung on wire, below, are an unusual and inexpensive garland idea for lights, trees, mantels, and banisters. This is a good opportunity to raid grandmother's button collection to display them so everyone can enjoy and perhaps reminisce about outfits that buttons may have come from. Use 26-gauge wire on a bolt and wire cutters. Cut the wire to desired length and make a closed loop on one end with needle-nosed pliers. Thread buttons onto the wire on the other end. Space buttons as desired. Hold buttons in position by making a single twist in the wire behind the button and flatten it against the button. When the length of wire is filled, make a closed loop on the open end to secure buttons. Hang the garland as desired.

Sentimental Display

This skinny metal tree, shown on the opposite page was originally white but was spray-painted with ivory silk-flower paint for an older look. It was decorated with a special emphasis on using unexpected elements such as old photographs, rhinestone pieces, lamp crystals, beads, baubles, and newsprint. Spend an evening cutting, wiring, and gluing away. It would be especially sentimental to decorate using old family photographs. Antique lace curtains frame the special tree that is displayed in the dining room.

Lights of the Season

An ordinary vintage chandelier, above, is fabulous with years of green patina. Pearl buttons were strung on thin, rusty wire to drape the branches in place of expensive crystals. Each

Vintage Memories

Use your imagination to see Simply Vintage Christmas decorations in everyday items. Shown at left, scrapbook letter tags hang from antique tinsel. A crystal salt shaker is wired with additional crystals and hung as an ornament. Sepia-toned photographs taken from old family albums like the one above are displayed in tiny picture frames and add that touch of aged brown to the decorating scheme. This is a particularly effective way of using family photographs as decorations. Take the photographs to a photocopy center and have sepia-toned color photocopies of your pictures made in the sizes of the frames you intend to use. Be certain the frames relate in color. Trim photographs and place in the frames. Make or buy ornament hangers and attach to frames, then hang from the tree's branches.

A small glitter cone, shown at left, is filled with old stamps, and letters from new scrapbooking materials. Use a glitter cone as a gift container to hide special, unexpected treats on the tree, or fill them with holiday candy, then hang them on a neighbor's door or place on a coworker's desk.

Crystal Ornament

Hang this crystal ornament from a tree or lamp, or tie onto a package with decorative ribbon as a gift tag. Smaller versions can be hung from a chain or ribbon for an unusual necklace.

- Clear nail polish
- Craft scissors
- Craft glue
- Emery board
- Flat paintbrush
- Glue stick
- Flat-sided teardrop lamp crystal, large
- Ornament hook
- Pencil
- Stamps, wallpaper scraps, or a color photocopy of a vintage photograph

1. Create a small collage using glue stick and stamps, wallpaper scraps, or color photocopy of a vintage photograph. *Note: Do not use an original; the paper is too thick for this project.*

2. Place collage under crystal and trace area to cut away. Trim paper to fit.

3. With paintbrush, coat flat area of crystal with craft glue.

4. Apply the right side of image or collage to glue so that it shows through front side of crystal. Let dry completely.

5. When dry, use an emery board to soften cut edges of paper slightly.

6. Coat back side of paper with clear nail polish.

7. Thread hook through hole and secure.

Right: Aged newsprint is cut with pinking shears into narrow strips, then fan-folded to be a unique garland on the tree.

About the Author

Sara Toliver joined the staff of Chapelle, Ltd., in 2002 as the company's Vice President, overseeing all marketing and publicity. She has the pleasure of working there with her mother, Jo Packham. She credits Jo with inspiring her every day to do more and to follow her dreams with every expectation that she can make them come true.

Sara went on to receive her MBA and together she and Jo opened three retail stores, of which Sara oversees the managerial, financial, and merchandising aspects. *Ruby & Begonia* was the recipient of back-to-back *Gifts & Decorative Accessories* Retailer Excellence Awards, winning the 2002 Gold Award for Excellence in Visual Merchandising and the 2003 Gold Award for Excellence in Community Service. Next they opened *The White Fig*, a most unusual gift basket company, and *Olive & Dahlia*, a garden decor and floral extravaganza.

Sara lives in Ogden with her wonderful and supportive husband, Brett, in a community that they both love. She participates in numerous volunteer and civic organizations, and as Vice President of the Historic 25th Street Merchants Association, she has had the opportunity to play an instrumental role in the redevelopment of that historic street. Sara and Jo together have authored *Ruby & Begonia's Christmas Style, Ruby & Begonia's Decorating Style,* and an upcoming gift basket book from *The White Fig*.

About Curious Sofa

Years ago when Debbie Dusenberry got her first apartment, flea-market decorating came out of financial necessity. For 19 years she worked as a photo stylist for photographers and directors in advertising, video, and motion pictures. Four years ago Debbie opened The Curious Sofa, in the gallery district of downtown Kansas City.

Her home is a mixture of natural linen slipcovers, rusty metal lawn furniture, animal-skin rugs, mirrors, and paintings—textures that goes with any season, and look especially great during Christmas. Her approach to decorating for the holidays is "less is more," and her home is so beautiful that it had to be included in our Simply Vintage chapter.

Metric Conversion Chart

mm-millimeters   cm-centimeters
inches to millimeters and centimeters

inches	mm	cm	inches	cm	inches	cm
⅛	3	0.3	9	22.9	30	76.2
¼	6	0.6	10	25.4	31	78.7
½	13	1.3	12	30.5	33	83.8
⅝	16	1.6	13	33.0	34	86.4
¾	19	1.9	14	35.6	35	88.9
⅞	22	2.2	15	38.1	36	91.4
1	25	2.5	16	40.6	37	94.0
1¼	32	3.2	17	43.2	38	96.5
1½	38	3.8	18	45.7	39	99.1
1¾	44	4.4	19	48.3	40	101.6
2	51	5.1	20	50.8	41	104.1
2½	64	6.4	21	53.3	42	106.7
3	76	7.6	22	55.9	43	109.2
3½	89	8.9	23	58.4	44	111.8
4	102	10.2	24	61.0	45	114.3
4½	114	11.4	25	63.5	46	116.8
5	127	12.7	26	66.0	47	119.4
6	152	15.2	27	68.6	48	121.9
7	178	17.8	28	71.1	49	124.5
8	203	20.3	29	73.7	50	127.0

yards to meters

yards	meters	yards	meters	yards	meters	yards	meters	yards	meters
⅛	0.11	2⅛	1.94	4⅛	3.77	6⅛	5.60	8⅛	7.43
¼	0.23	2¼	2.06	4¼	3.89	6¼	5.72	8¼	7.54
⅜	0.34	2⅜	2.17	4⅜	4.00	6⅜	5.83	8⅜	7.66
½	0.46	2½	2.29	4½	4.11	6½	5.94	8½	7.77
⅝	0.57	2⅝	2.40	4⅝	4.23	6⅝	6.06	8⅝	7.89
¾	0.69	2¾	2.51	4¾	4.34	6¾	6.17	8¾	8.00
⅞	0.80	2⅞	2.63	4⅞	4.46	6⅞	6.29	8⅞	8.12
1	0.91	3	2.74	5	4.57	7	6.40	9	8.23
1⅛	1.03	3⅛	2.86	5⅛	4.69	7⅛	6.52	9⅛	8.34
1¼	1.14	3¼	2.97	5¼	4.80	7¼	6.63	9¼	8.46
1⅜	1.26	3⅜	3.09	5⅜	4.91	7⅜	6.74	9⅜	8.57
1½	1.37	3½	3.20	5½	5.03	7½	6.86	9½	8.69
1⅝	1.49	3⅝	3.31	5⅝	5.14	7⅝	6.97	9⅝	8.80
1¾	1.60	3¾	3.43	5¾	5.26	7¾	7.09	9¾	8.92
1⅞	1.71	3⅞	3.54	5⅞	5.37	7⅞	7.20	9⅞	9.03
2	1.83	4	3.66	6	5.49	8	7.32	10	9.14

Acknowledgments

These are some of the resources used by our designers in creating the projects in this book:

Aldik
page 127, silver tree set

Backporch Friends
page 138 (LL) glitter cone

Bethany Lowe
16655 County Highway 16
Osco, IL 61274
800-944-6213
page 8 large clown
pages 73, 105 star box
page 90 (UR) angel, balls, star
page 91 (UL) moon Santa
page 105 (R) star box

Dept. 56
One Village Place
6436 City West Pkwy
Eden Prairie, MN 55344
page 73 (LL) large star

Greg Johnson
pages 7, 130, 132, gift wrapping

Jeremie
1356 Chattahoochee Ave., N.W.
Atlanta, GA 30318
404-875-3593
page 66 (LL) crystal beaded spheres

Laurie Fraser
page 133 (R), stocking
page 135 wool pillow

Midwest of Cannon Falls
P.O. Box 20
Cannon Falls, MN 55009
507-263-4261
page 8 medium and small clowns
page 54, 66 (UR), church box
page 84, primitive figurines
pages 85 (C), 89, 90 (LR), Santa
pages 92, 126 (LL), houses

Mosaics: Beyond the Basics
by Elizabeth DuVall
pages 117–119 Mirror Antiquing instructions

Quilted Projects for a Country Christmas
by Connie Duran
page 86 gift tag
page 108–109 Christmas Memories Collage instructions

Raz Imports
1017 East Loop 820
South Fort Worth, TX 76112
800-443-3540
page 26 papier-mâché boot

Squirrel Hill
20 Palatine #105
Irvine, CA 92612
949-955-3655
page 67 bottle-brush trees

Stickos
page 138 scrapbook letters

Wendy Addison for Chronicle Books
pages 124, 128, 129 (UL), 132 alphabet disks

Photography

Ryne Hazen: 4, 8–9, 11 (C), 12, 14–17, 22 (UR), 25–26, 28, 32, 54–58, 60, 64–74, 76, 78, 80–93, 97–98, 100, 103–109, 112 (UR), 114 (UL), 141, 143–144

Reprinted by permission of Hearst Communications, Inc.:
6, 115–116, 120 (R), 123
Photography by Toshi Otsuki: 1–3, 111 (C), 120 (L), 121, 122 (LC)
Photography by Starr Ockenga: 5, 110, 111 (L and C), 112 (L), 113, 114 (LL),

Jesse Walker: 10, 11 (L and R), 13, 22 (LL), 23–24, 33–45, 46 (L), 47–51

Nicole Cawlfield: 7, 124–139

Index